SECOND EDITION

THE SECOND COMING OF CHRIST

BASIC BIBLE DOCTRINES OF THE CHRISTIAN FAITH

Edward D. Andrews

THE SECOND COMING OF CHRIST

Basic Bible Doctrines of the Christian Faith

Edward D. Andrews

Christian Publishing House

Cambridge, Ohio

CHRISTIAN
PUBLISHING
HOUSE

FOUNDED 2005

THE SECOND COMING OF CHRIST: *Basic Bible Doctrines of the Christian Faith* by Edward D. Andrews

ISBN-10: 0692611134

ISBN-13: 978-0692611135

Table of Contents

PREFACE

Why the Second Coming Matters

The return of Jesus Christ stands at the center of the Christian hope. From the earliest days of the congregation, believers lived with the conviction that the risen and exalted Messiah would one day appear again in power and glory. This expectation was not a vague religious sentiment or a symbolic way of speaking about spiritual renewal. It was a concrete promise given by the Lord Himself and repeated by the apostles with clarity and urgency. The same Jesus who ascended into heaven will return in the same historical reality in which He departed, and His appearing will bring the present age of rebellion to its appointed end.

Yet few doctrines of the Bible have suffered more confusion than the doctrine of Christ's return. Throughout history, speculation has repeatedly replaced careful biblical interpretation. Some have turned the subject into endless predictions and timetables. Others have dismissed it as symbolic language describing the gradual progress of religion. Still others have fragmented the return of Christ into complicated systems of secret comings, hidden events, and speculative prophetic charts that often distract readers from the clear teaching of Scripture. None of these approaches does justice to the Word of God.

This book has been written with a simple conviction: the only safe guide in the study of the Second Coming is the Bible itself. Scripture must define the subject. Scripture must establish the sequence of events. Scripture must determine the meaning of prophetic language. When the testimony of the prophets, Jesus, the apostles, and the book of Revelation is allowed to speak in its own voice, the doctrine becomes far clearer than many assume.

The purpose of this book is therefore not to promote speculation but to restore biblical clarity. The return of Christ is presented in the New Testament as a visible, public, and world-shaking event. It is the moment when the present rebellion against God is judged, when the man of lawlessness and the beastly order are destroyed, when the faithful are vindicated, and when the kingdom of God advances toward its final fulfillment. The Second Coming is not an isolated event detached from the rest of biblical teaching. It stands at the center of a sequence of realities that includes resurrection, judgment, the defeat of evil powers, the reign of Christ, and the final renewal of creation.

A proper understanding of the Second Coming also depends upon recognizing the unity of the biblical witness. Daniel lays the prophetic groundwork by describing the rise and fall of empires, the persecution of the holy ones, and the final triumph of God's kingdom. Jesus expands these themes in His teaching about the end of the age. Paul explains the relationship between apostasy, the man of lawlessness, and the appearing of Christ. Revelation unveils the final confrontation between the Lamb and the rebellious powers of the world. When these passages are interpreted together through the historical-grammatical method, they form a coherent and consistent picture rather than a collection of disconnected predictions.

One of the most important aspects of this biblical framework is the connection between the return of Christ and the resurrection of the dead. The hope set before believers in the New Testament is not the survival of an immortal soul apart from the body. It is resurrection—God's act of restoring life through the power of the risen

Christ. The Second Coming marks the moment when this promise begins to unfold in its fullest sense. Those who belong to Christ will share in the resurrection life He secured through His victory over death, and the faithful will inherit the life God has prepared for His people.

Another important theme addressed in this book is the distinction between the holy ones who share in the first resurrection and reign with Christ and the broader righteous who receive everlasting life under God's kingdom. This distinction emerges from the combined testimony of Scripture, particularly in passages dealing with the first resurrection and the reign of Christ in Revelation. Recognizing this biblical structure helps clarify how the kingdom administration functions during the period of Christ's reign and how God's purposes for humanity reach their fulfillment.

At the same time, the doctrine of Christ's return is never given merely to satisfy curiosity about the future. The apostles consistently connect the Second Coming with the believer's present life. The certainty that Christ will appear again calls believers to faithfulness, endurance, holiness, and hope. The promise of His coming strengthens those who suffer, corrects those who drift from the truth, and reminds the church that the final word belongs not to the powers of this world but to the risen Lord.

For that reason, this book seeks to approach the subject with both seriousness and restraint. It avoids speculative theories and sensational predictions, focusing instead on the plain meaning of the biblical text. The aim is to present the doctrine of the Second Coming as the apostles presented it—clear enough to strengthen faith, serious enough to command attention, and hopeful enough to encourage perseverance.

The final message of Scripture is not uncertainty about the future but confidence in the triumph of Christ. The rebellious systems of the world may appear powerful for a time, but they are temporary. The kingdoms of this world do not have the last word. Jesus Christ does. He will appear. Evil will be judged. The faithful will be vindicated. And the purposes of God will stand forever.

It is my prayer that this study will help readers approach the subject of Christ's return with renewed clarity and confidence, grounded not in speculation but in the enduring authority of the Word of God.

Edward D. Andrews

Author of over 220 books and Chief Translator of the Updated American Standard Version (UASV)

INTRODUCTION

Understanding the Return of Jesus Christ

The return of Jesus Christ is one of the most central doctrines of the Christian faith. From the earliest proclamation of the gospel, believers were taught not only that Christ had died and been raised, but that He would come again. The apostles did not treat this expectation as a minor theological detail or a distant possibility. They presented it as a certainty rooted in the promises of God and confirmed by the resurrection and exaltation of Jesus Christ. The same Lord who ascended into heaven will return in glory, bringing the present age of rebellion to its appointed conclusion and establishing the next stage of God's kingdom purpose.

The New Testament repeatedly emphasizes that the return of Christ will be a visible and unmistakable event. Jesus Himself warned His disciples not to be misled by claims that His coming would be hidden, secret, or confined to private revelations. Instead, He described His coming as something that would be openly manifested, like lightning flashing across the sky. The apostles carried this same message forward. They taught that Christ would appear from heaven with power, that the dead would be raised, that the rebellious powers of the world would be judged, and that the faithful would share in the life and kingdom promised by God.

Despite the clarity of these teachings, the doctrine of the Second Coming has often been surrounded by confusion. Some have turned biblical prophecy into speculation about headlines, technologies, and political movements. Others have attempted to construct elaborate systems that divide Christ's return into multiple secret phases or hidden events. Still others have treated prophetic language as purely symbolic, denying that the Bible speaks of real historical events yet to come. These approaches have frequently obscured the straightforward message of Scripture.

This book seeks to approach the subject differently. The goal is not to advance speculative theories or to create a complicated prophetic system. Instead, the aim is to examine the biblical teaching about the return of Christ through the historical-grammatical method of interpretation. This means allowing Scripture to define its own terms, respecting the original context of prophetic passages, and reading the Bible as a unified revelation from God.

When Scripture is approached in this way, the doctrine of the Second Coming emerges with remarkable coherence. The prophetic visions of Daniel describe the rise of earthly empires, the persecution of the holy ones, and the final triumph of the kingdom of God. The teaching of Jesus expands these themes, warning His disciples about deception, tribulation, and the visible arrival of the Son of Man. Paul explains how the great apostasy and the man of lawlessness fit into the unfolding of the last days and how Christ will destroy that lawless power by the appearance of His coming. The book of Revelation then provides a panoramic view of the final conflict between the Lamb and the rebellious powers of the world, culminating in the defeat of evil, the reign of Christ, and the ultimate renewal of creation.

Together these passages form a consistent biblical framework. Christ returns. The rebellious order that opposes God is judged and removed. Satan's power is restrained. The faithful are raised and vindicated. The kingdom of God advances toward its final fulfillment. These events are not disconnected pieces of prophecy but parts of one unfolding divine purpose.

A proper understanding of the Second Coming also requires attention to the biblical doctrine of resurrection. The Christian hope is not based on the idea that the human soul possesses natural immortality. Instead, the hope of the believer is resurrection through the power of God. Just as Christ was raised from the dead, so those who belong to Him will be raised when He appears. The victory of Christ over death is the foundation of the believer's future life.

The Scriptures also speak of a particular resurrection described as the first resurrection, associated with those who share in Christ's reign. This reality is closely connected with the kingdom themes that run throughout prophecy. At the same time, the Bible promises everlasting life to the righteous under God's kingdom. Understanding these themes within their biblical framework helps clarify the structure of God's redemptive plan and prevents confusion about the nature of the hope set before believers.

The purpose of studying the Second Coming is not merely to understand future events. Scripture consistently connects the return of Christ with the believer's present life. The expectation that Christ will appear again calls believers to watchfulness, faithfulness, and perseverance. It reminds the church that evil does not have the final word in history. The world may be filled with injustice, rebellion, and suffering, but the return of Christ assures believers that God's purposes will prevail.

For this reason, the doctrine of the Second Coming has always been a source of encouragement for Christians. It reminds believers that the story of redemption is moving toward a definite conclusion. The promises of God will not fail. The kingdom announced by the prophets and proclaimed by Jesus will reach its fulfillment. The risen Lord who reigns now in heaven will one day appear openly, and when He does, the triumph of God's purpose will be revealed for all to see.

This study is therefore offered with a simple objective: to examine the biblical teaching about the return of Jesus Christ in a clear, careful, and faithful way. By allowing Scripture to interpret Scripture and by focusing on the central themes revealed in the prophetic and apostolic writings, readers can approach the subject with confidence rather than confusion.

The hope of the church has always been expressed in a simple and powerful confession: Jesus Christ is coming again. The pages that follow seek to explore what the Bible teaches about that promise and why it remains one of the most important doctrines of the Christian faith.

Chapter 1 — The Central Hope of Biblical Christianity

The Return of Christ at the Center of the Christian Faith

The Second Coming of Christ stands at the very center of biblical Christianity. It is not a minor doctrine reserved for speculative discussion, nor is it an optional theme for readers especially interested in prophecy. It is woven into the fabric of the New Testament proclamation. Jesus spoke of His return openly and repeatedly. The apostles preached it as a certainty. The early congregations lived in the light of it. The church's hope was never grounded in human progress, religious institutions, or political reform, but in the personal return of the risen and exalted Lord Jesus Christ.

The New Testament does not present believers as merely looking back to the cross and resurrection, though those remain foundational to redemption. It also presents them as looking forward. Paul writes that believers "wait for His Son from heaven, whom He raised from the dead, Jesus, who rescues us from the coming wrath" (1 Thess. 1:10). He describes Christians as those who are "awaiting our blessed hope, the appearing of the glory of our great God and Savior Jesus Christ" (Titus 2:13). He declares that the Savior "will transform the body of our humble state into conformity with the body of His glory" (Phil. 3:20–21). Peter speaks of an "inheritance incorruptible and undefiled and unfading, reserved in heaven for you" and connects that hope with "the revelation of Jesus Christ" (1 Pet. 1:4–7, 13). John says, "we know that whenever He is made manifest, we will be like Him, because we will see Him just as He is" (1 John 3:2). These are not scattered references. They reveal the settled expectation of the apostolic church.

The New Testament church therefore did not treat the return of Christ as an appendix to the faith. It was part of the faith's living heartbeat. Believers endured persecution because Christ would return. They resisted deception because Christ would return. They buried their dead in hope because Christ would return. They preached, worshiped, and persevered in the certainty that history was moving toward the appearing of the King. This is why Paul could comfort grieving believers, not by directing them to an immortal soul already enjoying conscious bliss, but by directing them to the return of Christ and the resurrection of the dead at His coming (1 Thess. 4:13–18; 1 Cor. 15:20–23).

The centrality of this doctrine also appears in the language the New Testament uses to describe Christian life. Believers are those who "love His appearing" (2 Tim. 4:8).

They are those who "wait eagerly" for the Lord from heaven (Phil. 3:20). They are those who "wait for the revealing of our Lord Jesus Christ" (1 Cor. 1:7). Their hope is not escape into a bodiless state, nor does Scripture teach that all the redeemed receive the same future reward in the same form. The return of Christ brings resurrection, judgment, and kingdom fulfillment. The select holy ones who reign with Christ receive immortality in the heavenly calling (1 Cor. 15:53–54; Rev. 20:4–6), while the broader righteous receive eternal life under God's kingdom (John 3:16; Matt. 25:46). That is why the Second Coming cannot be pushed to the margins without distorting the shape of biblical Christianity itself.

The Hope Announced by Jesus, the Apostles, and the Prophets

The expectation of Christ's return rests on the united witness of Scripture. The prophets laid the foundation by speaking of Jehovah's coming in judgment, the reign of the Messiah, the overthrow of arrogant world power, and the final vindication of the faithful. Psalm 2 speaks of the nations raging against Jehovah and against His Anointed, only to be broken under Messiah's rule (Ps. 2:1–12). Isaiah foretells the reign of the coming King whose government and peace will increase without end (Isa. 9:6–7), and he speaks of a future day when Jehovah will swallow up death forever and wipe tears from all faces (Isa. 25:8). Daniel sees the Son of Man receiving everlasting dominion and a kingdom that will not be destroyed (Dan. 7:13–14), and he speaks of the resurrection of the dead and the final division between everlasting life and everlasting contempt (Dan. 12:2–3). Zechariah foretells the day when Jehovah will stand in decisive intervention against the nations and reign as King over all the earth (Zech. 14:3–9).

These prophecies do not end with the humiliation of the Messiah. They require His reign. They require His public triumph. They require the overthrow of rebellious power and the establishment of God's kingdom in history. The prophets therefore laid down the categories that the New Testament later unfolds with greater clarity.

Jesus did not diminish those expectations. He confirmed and intensified them. In the Olivet Discourse He warned of deception, wars, persecution, apostasy, and tribulation, and then declared that "they will see the Son of Man coming on the clouds of heaven with power and great glory" (Matt. 24:30). He said He would send forth His angels with a great trumpet, and they would gather His chosen ones (Matt. 24:31). He connected His coming with judgment in the parables of the faithful and evil slave, the ten virgins, the talents, and the sheep and goats (Matt. 24:45–25:46). He declared before the high priest that they would see "the Son of Man sitting at the right hand of Power and coming on the clouds of heaven" (Matt. 26:64). He taught not merely survival of a message, but His own return as Lord and Judge.

The apostles preached the same hope. The angels told the disciples at the ascension, "This Jesus who has been taken up from you into heaven will come in just the same way as you have watched Him go into heaven" (Acts 1:11). Peter proclaimed that heaven must receive Christ "until the times of restoration of all things" spoken by the prophets (Acts 3:21). Paul taught that "the Lord Himself will descend from heaven" (1 Thess. 4:16), that the lawless one will be destroyed "by the appearance of His coming" (2 Thess. 2:8), and that Christ must reign until every enemy, including death, is put under His feet (1 Cor. 15:23–26). James urged believers to be patient "until the presence of the Lord" and declared that "the presence of the Lord has drawn near"

(Jas. 5:7–8). Peter warned that scoffers would deny the promise of His coming, yet he insisted that the day of the Lord would come and that believers must therefore live in holiness and expectation (2 Pet. 3:3–14). John wrote, "Look, He is coming with the clouds, and every eye will see Him" (Rev. 1:7).

The doctrine is therefore not a construction built on a handful of obscure verses. It is the unified testimony of prophets, Jesus, and apostles. The whole biblical witness moves toward the same climax: Jesus Christ will return.

The Return of Christ Is Literal, Visible, and Historical

The Second Coming of Christ must be understood as a literal, visible, historical event. Scripture does not present it as a mere symbol of spiritual victory, a gradual triumph of gospel influence, an invisible coming into the believer's heart, or a secret removal of the church from the earth. It presents a return as real as His first coming, His death, His resurrection, and His ascension.

Acts 1:11 is decisive: "This Jesus who has been taken up from you into heaven will come in just the same way as you have watched Him go into heaven." The ascension was not invisible, symbolic, or inward. The disciples saw Him go. The angelic promise therefore requires a corresponding return. In Matthew 24:27 Jesus said, "just as the lightning comes from the east and shines as far as the west, so the presence of the Son of Man will be." That image excludes secrecy. Lightning is public, sudden, unmistakable. Revelation 1:7 is equally clear: "every eye will see Him." Paul says that the Lord will descend "with a shout, with the voice of an archangel and with the trumpet of God" (1 Thess. 4:16). That language does not describe an invisible event. It describes divine intervention that is public, audible, and glorious. The same pattern is reflected in 2 Thessalonians 2:8, where the lawless one is brought to nothing "by the appearance of His coming." The appearance is not hidden. It is the unveiled manifestation of Christ's authority. This visible, bodily, premillennial return preceding the reign is also the consistent sequence stated in the Pauline material and the Revelation material already established in the uploaded works.

The New Testament also resists every attempt to divide Christ's return into multiple disconnected phases. Scripture speaks of one great appearing, one παρουσία, one revelation, one descent, one visible intervention in which the dead are raised, the living are transformed, the wicked are judged, and the kingdom moves into its next decisive phase (Matt. 24:29–31; 1 Thess. 4:16–17; 2 Thess. 1:7–10; 2 Thess. 2:8; 1 Cor. 15:23–26). The return of Christ is therefore not a hidden preliminary event followed later by a public event. It is the public event.

To say that the Second Coming is historical is equally important. Scripture does not treat it as timeless religious symbolism. It belongs to the movement of redemptive history. Christ entered history in His first coming, was crucified under Pontius Pilate, was raised bodily, ascended visibly, and now reigns at the right hand of God. The same Jesus who acted in history will return in history. His coming will not merely alter private religious feeling. It will end the present age in its current rebellious form, bring resurrection, execute judgment, destroy the anti-God order, and inaugurate the next stage of divine kingdom administration.

Edward D. Andrews

The Blessed Hope of the Early Church

The New Testament church lived in the expectation of Christ's return because that hope gave shape to every other doctrine. It gave meaning to suffering. It gave urgency to holiness. It gave courage to evangelism. It gave substance to resurrection hope. It gave perspective to the rise of evil and the arrogance of human power.

Paul's words to the Thessalonians are especially instructive. He did not soothe them with philosophical reflections about the immortality of the soul. He directed them to the return of Christ. "For if we believe that Jesus died and rose again, in the same way also God will bring with Him those who have fallen asleep through Jesus" (1 Thess. 4:14). He then explains the sequence: the Lord descends, the dead in Christ rise first, then the living are gathered together with them to meet the Lord (1 Thess. 4:16–17). The comfort is resurrection at Christ's return, not conscious existence apart from the body. Yet resurrection itself must be understood carefully. Scripture distinguishes between immortality and eternal life. Immortality is the indestructible life granted to those called to reign with Christ (1 Cor. 15:53–54; Rev. 20:4–6), whereas eternal life is the unending life granted to the righteous under God's kingdom (John 3:16). The Christian hope, therefore, is not centered on escaping embodiment, but on the defeat of death through resurrection and the granting of the life God appoints to each class of the saved.

This expectation also made the church sober. The apostles never taught prophetic indifference. They taught watchfulness. Jesus said, "keep on the watch" (Matt. 24:42). Paul said, "let us not sleep as the rest do, but let us stay awake and keep our senses" (1 Thess. 5:6). Peter said that "the end of all things has drawn close," and therefore

20

believers must be of sound mind and watchful in prayer (1 Pet. 4:7). John said that everyone who has this hope fixed on Christ "purifies himself just as that one is pure" (1 John 3:3). This is not sensational excitement. It is moral seriousness produced by certainty that the King will return.

The church's worship was also marked by this expectation. Believers did not gather merely to remember a past act of redemption. They gathered to proclaim the Lord's death "until He comes" (1 Cor. 11:26). The Supper itself was therefore future-oriented. The congregation lived between accomplished redemption and coming consummation. The cross could not be severed from the crown, and justification could not be severed from resurrection and kingdom.

The Return of Christ and the End of the Present Age

The present age will not continue indefinitely. Scripture does not teach that evil will gradually disappear through human effort or that the nations will peacefully evolve into the kingdom of God. It teaches that the present order remains under corruption, deception, rebellion, and death until Christ intervenes in judgment and power.

Jesus connected His return with "the end of the age" (Matt. 24:3). In the explanation of the wheat and the weeds, He said that "the harvest is a conclusion of a system of things," and that at that time the Son of Man will send forth His angels, remove lawlessness, and gather the righteous into their appointed glory (Matt. 13:39–43). Paul likewise ties Christ's return to the destruction of the lawless one (2 Thess. 2:8), the resurrection of those who belong to Him (1 Cor. 15:23), and the progressive defeat of all enemies, climaxing in the destruction of death itself (1 Cor. 15:24–

26). Peter says that the present heavens and earth are reserved for judgment and that the day of the Lord will arrive with irreversible consequences for the present wicked order (2 Pet. 3:7–13).

This means the return of Christ is not only the believer's comfort. It is also the crisis of the world. The same event that gathers the faithful exposes the wicked. The same appearing that raises the dead in Christ brings ruin upon the anti-God order. The New Testament never separates salvation and judgment at the appearing of Christ. He comes to save His people and to judge His enemies. That is why the doctrine cannot be softened into a vague message of inspiration. It is the decisive intervention of the Son of God in history.

At the same time, Scripture does not present the return of Christ as the end of all divine purpose beyond that point. It is the end of the present age in its rebellious form, but it also initiates the next phase of Christ's kingdom rule. Revelation 19–20 places the appearing of Christ before the thousand-year reign, not after it, and therefore the Second Coming stands as the beginning of the millennial kingdom, not as a symbol for the whole present age or as an event after the kingdom has already run its course. The sequence of Christ's victory over the beastly order, Satan's binding, and the thousand-year reign is part of the fixed doctrinal structure already laid down in the uploaded Revelation material.

The Return of Christ and the Beginning of His Reign

Biblical Christianity does not merely look for an ending. It looks for a King. The Second Coming is not simply the termination of one era. It is the open manifestation of Christ's royal authority over the nations. The New Testament repeatedly presents Jesus as already exalted and reigning at the right hand of God (Ps. 110:1; Acts 2:33–36; 1 Cor. 15:25; Heb. 1:3, 13). Yet the same Scriptures also teach that there remains a future public manifestation of that reign in relation to His enemies, the nations, the resurrection, and the judgment of the world.

The imagery of Daniel and Revelation is essential here. Daniel saw the Son of Man receive dominion, glory, and a kingdom so that all peoples should serve Him (Dan. 7:13–14). Revelation presents the Lamb as worthy to take the scroll and carry out the decreed purposes of God (Rev. 5:1–10). It presents Christ later appearing as the rider on the white horse who judges and wages war in righteousness (Rev. 19:11–16). It then places the binding of Satan and the thousand-year reign after that victory (Rev. 20:1–6). The kingdom, therefore, is not an afterthought tacked onto the doctrine of the Second Coming. The return of Christ is the transition point by which the present rebellious order is decisively broken and the millennial reign is inaugurated. That premillennial sequence is one of the strongest points of continuity between the present book and the already established material on Paul and Revelation.

This is why the Second Coming must be described as central hope rather than speculative appendage. The return of Christ is the hinge on which resurrection, judgment, kingdom, and restoration all turn. Without it, the church has no biblical basis for expecting the defeat of death, the overthrow of the anti-God order, or the open triumph of righteousness in God's appointed future.

Edward D. Andrews

The Church Must Reject Speculative Systems and Sensationalism

Because the doctrine of Christ's return is so central, it has often been abused. Scripture itself warns of deception in the last days and of false claims concerning the nearness or form of Christ's coming (Matt. 24:4–5, 23–27; 2 Thess. 2:1–3; 2 Pet. 3:3–4). Some have turned the doctrine into sensational timetables. Others have reduced it to symbolic language about cultural change or inward spirituality. Still others have divided Christ's coming into elaborate systems not grounded in the text itself. None of these approaches does justice to the biblical witness.

The New Testament never encourages date-setting. Jesus said plainly, "concerning that day and hour nobody knows" (Matt. 24:36). Acts 1:7 says that the Father has set times and seasons by His own authority. The duty of believers is therefore not speculative certainty about hidden chronology, but watchfulness, faithfulness, and discernment. Paul warned the Thessalonians not to be quickly shaken by claims that the day had already come (2 Thess. 2:1–3). Peter warned that scoffers would mock the promise of Christ's coming, but he did not answer them with sensationalism. He answered them with the certainty of divine judgment and the call to holy conduct (2 Pet. 3:3–14).

Scripture also opposes the reduction of the doctrine to inward or invisible categories. Christ's return is not the gradual spread of Christian influence. It is not His coming in the destruction of Jerusalem alone. It is not His coming in the believer's devotional experience. It is not a secret removal of the church before tribulation. It is the appearing of the Lord Himself, in glory, with resurrection, judgment, and kingdom consequences. The apostolic pattern is clear:

apostasy and lawlessness mature, Christ appears, evil is judged, the dead are raised, and the kingdom moves into its next revealed stage (2 Thess. 2:3–8; 1 Cor. 15:23–26; Rev. 19–20). That doctrinal sequence has already been treated explicitly in the Pauline and apocalyptic material now guiding this project.

Modern sensationalism also tends to fixate on identifying technologies, political figures, or current events while neglecting the theological center of prophecy. But biblical prophecy is first about Christ, His kingdom, His judgment, and His victory. It is also about worship, allegiance, perseverance, and holiness. End-time speculation that leaves believers fearful, unstable, or obsessed with novelty has already departed from the pastoral purpose of Scripture. The prophetic word was given so that believers would remain faithful, not so that they would become captive to endless excitement.

The Second Coming as the Hope That Purifies and Strengthens

Because the return of Christ is certain, it reshapes the whole Christian life. It teaches believers how to suffer, because present affliction is neither ultimate nor endless. It teaches them how to resist compromise, because the present age is passing away. It teaches them how to grieve, because death itself will be overturned in resurrection. It teaches them how to worship, because the Lamb who was slain will reign openly. It teaches them how to endure, because the final word belongs not to beastly power, false religion, or lawless rebellion, but to Jesus Christ.

This hope purifies. "Everyone who has this hope fixed on Him purifies himself just as that one is pure" (1 John 3:3). The church that truly waits for Christ cannot live comfortably in moral compromise. The certainty of His appearing presses upon conscience. It exposes false security. It calls for repentance, vigilance, and steadfast obedience.

This hope also steadies. Paul closes his great passage on resurrection not with speculation, but with exhortation: "Therefore, my beloved brothers, be steadfast, immovable, always having plenty to do in the work of the Lord, knowing that your labor is not in vain in the Lord" (1 Cor. 15:58). The certainty of resurrection and Christ's victory produces endurance in present labor. What is done in loyalty to Christ is not wasted. History is not closed by the power of death. It is opened by the return of the living Lord.

This hope finally exalts Christ Himself. The New Testament church did not merely await events. It awaited a Person. The object of hope is not chronology, not escape, not speculation, but Jesus Christ. The church says, in effect, what Revelation says openly: "Amen. Come, Lord Jesus" (Rev. 22:20). That is the language of biblical Christianity. It is the language of a faith that knows its Redeemer lives, that He reigns now, that He will appear, and that when He appears the present age will reach its appointed end and His righteous kingdom will advance openly under the decree of Jehovah.

Chapter 2 — Old Testament Foundations of the Coming King

The Second Coming Rooted in the Prophets

The Second Coming of Christ is not a doctrine created in the New Testament. It is the fulfillment of a hope already embedded in the Old Testament Scriptures. The prophets did not merely speak of a coming Savior who would suffer, die, and redeem. They also spoke of a coming King who would reign, judge, deliver, and establish the kingdom of God in open triumph. The New Testament does not invent that expectation. It identifies Jesus Christ as the One in whom those ancient promises find their fulfillment.

Edward D. Andrews

This is why the doctrine of Christ's return cannot be treated as a peripheral development of later Christian theology. It is rooted in the promises Jehovah made through the Law, the Psalms, and the Prophets. The Old Testament repeatedly looks beyond the present order of sin, rebellion, and Gentile dominion to a future intervention of God through His Anointed. It speaks of a kingdom that will not be destroyed, of a righteous ruler who will govern the nations, of the overthrow of arrogant world power, of the vindication of the faithful, and of a renewed creation under divine rule. Those expectations require more than the first coming of Christ. They require His return in glory.

The prophets present the Messiah in two major lines of revelation. One line speaks of His humiliation, rejection, suffering, and sacrificial work. The other speaks of His royal majesty, victorious reign, judgment of the wicked, and restoration of the faithful. These lines are not contradictory. They belong to the same Messiah. But they are not exhausted in one historical moment. The suffering Messiah came first. The reigning Messiah must yet come in the full public manifestation of His kingdom. Thus the Old Testament itself creates the expectation that the Messiah's work will unfold in more than one stage, though the prophets themselves often place those realities side by side in compressed prophetic vision.

The Psalms and the Promise of the Reigning Son

The Psalms provide some of the clearest Old Testament foundations for the coming kingship of the Messiah. Psalm 2 is fundamental. The nations rage and the peoples devise vain things against Jehovah and against His Anointed, saying, "Let us tear their bonds apart and cast away their cords from us" (Ps. 2:1–3). But Jehovah responds from heaven with derision, declaring, "I have installed my King upon Zion, my holy mountain" (Ps. 2:6). The Son is then told, "Ask of me, and I will certainly give the nations as your inheritance, and the ends of the earth as your possession. You shall break them with an iron scepter, you shall dash them in pieces like a potter's vessel" (Ps. 2:8–9).

This Psalm cannot be reduced to Davidic kingship in its original historical setting. Its language reaches beyond any ordinary king of Israel. The Son receives the nations, not merely Israel. He rules to the ends of the earth, not merely within a regional kingdom. He breaks rebellious rulers and demands universal submission. The New Testament repeatedly applies this Psalm to Christ (Acts 4:25–28; 13:33; Heb. 1:5; Rev. 2:26–27; 12:5; 19:15). But the full scope of Psalm 2 has not yet been exhausted in history. The nations still rage. The rulers of the earth still resist the Messiah. The promised breaking of rebellious kings in open judgment awaits the visible intervention of Christ. Psalm 2 therefore requires not only the exaltation of Christ but His future appearing as King over the nations.

Psalm 110 is equally decisive. Jehovah says to David's Lord, "Sit at my right hand until I make your enemies a footstool for your feet" (Ps. 110:1). This verse is cited repeatedly in the New Testament as describing Christ's present exaltation at the right hand of God (Matt. 22:44; Acts 2:34–36; Heb. 1:13). But the Psalm does not end with heavenly session. It continues: "Jehovah will stretch out the scepter of your strength from Zion, saying: 'Go subduing in the midst of your enemies'" (Ps. 110:2). It describes a priest-king after the order of Melchizedek (Ps. 110:4), and then speaks of judgment: "The Lord is at your right hand; He will shatter kings in the day of His wrath. He will execute judgment among the nations" (Ps. 110:5–6).

Again, the pattern is unmistakable. The Messiah is exalted first. He sits at Jehovah's right hand. But the Psalm also demands a future day of wrath and judgment in which kings are shattered and nations are brought under His rule. Christ's present heavenly reign does not remove the need for His future open intervention. Rather, it guarantees it. He reigns now in exalted authority, but Psalm 110 requires a future historical manifestation of that authority against His enemies. That manifestation belongs to the doctrine of the Second Coming.

Psalm 72 likewise extends beyond Solomon and points toward the greater Son of David. The king described there rules "from sea to sea and from the River to the ends of the earth" (Ps. 72:8). The desert tribes bow before Him, His enemies lick the dust, the kings of Tarshish and the islands bring gifts, and "all kings bow down before him; all nations serve him" (Ps. 72:9–11). He delivers the needy, has pity on the weak, and fills the earth with blessing (Ps. 72:12–19). No ordinary king of Israel fulfilled these universal terms. The Psalm reaches its true goal only in the Messiah. Yet the world has not yet seen all kings bow before Christ in open submission. That universal royal dominion still lies ahead. The Old Testament therefore points beyond the first coming toward the day when the Messiah's reign is openly manifested.

Isaiah and the Coming Kingdom of Righteousness

Isaiah develops the hope of the coming King with extraordinary fullness. In Isaiah 9:6–7 the prophet announces, "A child has been born to us, a son has been given to us; and the government will rest on his shoulder." He is called Wonderful Counselor, Mighty God, Eternal

Father, Prince of Peace, and "there will be no end to the increase of his government or of peace, on the throne of David and over his kingdom, to establish it and to uphold it with justice and righteousness from then on and forevermore."

The first part of the prophecy clearly speaks of the Messiah's coming into history as a child. Yet the passage does not stop with incarnation. It moves immediately to everlasting government, Davidic kingship, and unending peace. This cannot be exhausted by Christ's first coming alone. He did not sit upon David's throne in visible rule over the nations during His earthly ministry. Nor did His first coming bring the end of war, oppression, and rebellion in the world. The prophecy therefore requires the future establishment of His kingdom in manifested power. The zeal of Jehovah guarantees this outcome (Isa. 9:7), but the fulfillment reaches beyond Bethlehem to the glorious reign of the returning King.

Isaiah 11 continues the same line. A shoot comes forth from the stump of Jesse, and the Spirit of Jehovah rests upon Him in wisdom, understanding, counsel, and might (Isa. 11:1–2). He judges with righteousness, strikes the earth "with the rod of his mouth," and slays the wicked "with the breath of his lips" (Isa. 11:4–5). Then follows the vision of peace in creation, the gathering of the dispersed, and the knowledge of Jehovah filling the earth "as the waters cover the sea" (Isa. 11:6–12).

This chapter combines messianic identity, righteous judgment, destruction of the wicked, restoration of the faithful, and transformed creation. The New Testament applies the root of Jesse to Christ (Rom. 15:12), but the complete picture remains future. The earth is not yet full of the knowledge of Jehovah in the way Isaiah describes. The wicked have not yet been openly destroyed by the judicial power of the Messiah. The faithful from all quarters have not yet been gathered into the fully restored order under His reign. Isaiah 11 therefore points beyond the first coming to the Second Coming and kingdom reign of Christ.

Isaiah 25 is also crucial. Jehovah of armies prepares a feast for all peoples, removes the veil spread over the nations, "will swallow up death forever," and "will wipe tears away from all faces" (Isa. 25:6–8). This promise is later taken up in the New Testament in connection with resurrection and final victory (1 Cor. 15:54; Rev. 21:4). But the context in Isaiah is kingdom-centered. It is tied to Jehovah's public intervention, the vindication of His people, and the overthrow of the proud city opposed to Him. The swallowing up of death is not detached from God's reign. It belongs to the consummation that arrives through His victorious rule.

Isaiah 32 speaks of a king who "will reign in righteousness" and of princes who rule in justice (Isa. 32:1). Isaiah 42 presents Jehovah's Servant bringing forth justice to the nations (Isa. 42:1–4). Isaiah 52–53 reveals the suffering Servant who is marred, despised, pierced, and crushed for the sins of others (Isa. 52:13–53:12). Yet Isaiah does not end with suffering. The Servant is exalted, prospers, and justifies many. Isaiah's own structure therefore demands both humiliation and exaltation, suffering and reign, sacrifice and kingdom victory. The same Messiah who bears sin must also rule. Since the full open rule did not occur in His first coming, it must occur in His second.

Daniel and the Kingdom That Crushes All Others

No Old Testament book lays a stronger prophetic foundation for the Second Coming than Daniel. Daniel presents the course of world empire, the arrogance of beastly power, the heavenly court, the Son of Man, the resurrection of the dead, and the everlasting kingdom. The New Testament's doctrine of Christ's return stands in direct continuity with Daniel's prophetic structure.

Daniel 2 records Nebuchadnezzar's dream of the great image made of successive materials, representing successive kingdoms. Then a stone "cut out without hands" strikes the image, crushes it completely, and becomes "a great mountain and filled the whole earth" (Dan. 2:34–35). Daniel explains that in the days of those kings "the God of heaven will set up a kingdom that will never be destroyed," and it "will crush and put an end to all these kingdoms, but it will itself stand forever" (Dan. 2:44).

This is not the language of gradual moral improvement. It is the language of decisive intervention. The kingdoms of this world are not slowly absorbed by religious influence. They are struck, shattered, and replaced by the kingdom established by God. The stone does not symbolize a purely inward spiritual reality detached from history. It represents the kingdom of God arriving in judgment against the kingdom order of rebellious man. Since the kingdoms of human power still stand in open rebellion, Daniel 2 requires a future intervention by the Messiah in which that beastly order is decisively broken.

Daniel 7 intensifies the picture. Four great beasts arise from the sea, representing kingdoms (Dan. 7:3, 17). The final beast is dreadful, powerful, and destructive. A little horn arises speaking arrogant things and making war with the holy ones (Dan. 7:8, 21, 25). Then the scene shifts to heaven: "thrones were set up," the Ancient of Days takes His seat, the court sits in judgment, and the beast is destroyed (Dan. 7:9–11). After that, "with the clouds of heaven One like a Son of Man was coming," and to Him is given dominion, glory, and a kingdom, "that all peoples, nations, and men of every language might serve Him" (Dan. 7:13–14).

The Son of Man language is central to Jesus' own teaching about His return (Matt. 24:30; 26:64). Daniel 7 presents not only messianic authority but messianic judgment over beastly empire. The beast is destroyed, the arrogant horn is judged, and the Son of Man receives universal dominion. That universal dominion is then shared, in a derivative sense, with the holy ones of the Most High (Dan. 7:18, 27). The prophecy therefore demands a future point at which anti-God world power is judged and Christ's kingdom is openly established. The first coming did not bring the destruction of the final beastly order. The Second Coming must do so.

Daniel 12 confirms the same future orientation. Michael stands up in a time of distress unlike any before it, and at that time the people of God are delivered (Dan. 12:1). Then follows the resurrection: "many of those sleeping in the dust of the ground will awake, these to everlasting life, but the others to reproach and everlasting contempt" (Dan. 12:2). Here the pattern is unmistakable: final distress, divine intervention, deliverance, resurrection, and everlasting outcome. Daniel's wording is also important, for it speaks of everlasting life and not of immortality being granted alike to all. The fuller New Testament revelation will distinguish between the select resurrected holy ones who receive immortality for heavenly reign and the broader righteous who receive everlasting life under God's kingdom. Daniel therefore does not merely offer background color. It provides the prophetic architecture of the doctrine.

Zechariah and the Day of Jehovah

Zechariah adds another essential Old Testament witness to the coming King. The prophet combines the lowly first coming of the Messiah with the future day of His triumph. Zechariah 9:9 famously says, "Look! Your king is coming to you; he is righteous and endowed with salvation, humble, and mounted on a donkey." The New Testament rightly applies this to Jesus' entry into Jerusalem (Matt. 21:4–5; John 12:14–15). Yet the surrounding context does not end there. Zechariah 9 also speaks of dominion "from sea to sea and from the River to the ends of the earth" (Zech. 9:10). The King comes humbly, but His reign is universal. The first coming fulfills the lowly entrance. The second coming fulfills the worldwide dominion.

Zechariah 12 and 14 are especially important. In Zechariah 12:10 Jehovah says, "they will look on me whom they pierced; and they will mourn for him." The New Testament applies this to Christ (John 19:37; Rev. 1:7). But Zechariah does not stop with mourning. Chapter 14 describes the day when the nations gather against Jerusalem, Jehovah goes forth to fight, and "his feet will stand in that day on the Mount of Olives" (Zech. 14:3–4). The chapter continues with Jehovah becoming "King over all the earth" (Zech. 14:9).

The imagery is vivid, but its theological meaning is plain. The day of Jehovah is a day of intervention, warfare against rebellious nations, deliverance of the faithful, and kingship established. Since Revelation 1:7 combines the cloud-coming of the Son of Man with the mourning language of Zechariah 12, the New Testament itself teaches that these Zecharian themes belong to the return of Christ. The pierced One is the coming King, and His return means both judgment and reign.

The Suffering Messiah and the Reigning Messiah

A central Old Testament fact must be faced honestly: the prophets speak both of a suffering Messiah and of a reigning Messiah. Isaiah 53 presents the Servant despised, rejected, pierced, crushed, and bearing the sins of many. Psalm 22 speaks of the righteous sufferer whose hands and feet are pierced, whose garments are divided, and who is mocked by His enemies. Zechariah 12:10 speaks of the pierced One. Daniel 9:26 says the Messiah will be cut off. These texts are fulfilled in the humiliation, suffering, and death of Jesus Christ.

But the same Old Testament also speaks of the Messiah ruling the nations, judging the wicked, restoring the faithful, and reigning forever. Psalm 2, Psalm 72, Psalm 110, Isaiah 9, Isaiah 11, Daniel 7, and Zechariah 14 all require not merely redemptive suffering but royal triumph. The prophets often place these realities close together because they are looking at the one Messiah and the one divine purpose. But history reveals that those realities unfold in stages. The first coming accomplished the atoning work. The second coming will accomplish the public triumph of the kingdom.

This pattern is already visible in Jesus' own reading of Scripture. In Luke 4:18–21 He reads from Isaiah 61 but stops before the phrase concerning "the day of vengeance of our God." His first coming inaugurated the proclamation of good news, release, and divine favor. But the day of vengeance and kingdom judgment remained future. The same prophetic text contains both grace and judgment, first coming and second coming. This is not contradiction. It is prophetic compression resolved in the unfolding of redemptive history.

Therefore the Old Testament does not force a choice between suffering and reigning. It requires both. And since both are assigned to the one Messiah, the kingdom prophecies necessarily require a future return of Christ.

The Kingdom Promises Made to the Faithful

The promises made to the faithful in the Old Testament also require the future return of the Messiah. Abraham was promised not merely personal blessing but worldwide covenant fulfillment through his seed (Gen. 12:1–3; 22:18). David was promised an enduring throne and kingdom (2 Sam. 7:12–16; Ps. 89:3–4, 34–37). The righteous were promised inheritance of the earth (Ps. 37:9–11, 29). Daniel's holy ones were promised that they would receive the kingdom (Dan. 7:18, 27). Isaiah spoke of renewed creation and enduring peace under divine rule (Isa. 11:6–9; 65:17–25).

These promises have not yet reached their full historical realization. The faithful have often suffered, been oppressed, and died without seeing the visible kingdom fully established. Hebrews 11 explicitly says that many faithful ones died in faith without receiving the complete fulfillment of the promises, because God had provided something better in the forward-moving plan of redemption (Heb. 11:13, 39–40). Their hope therefore remained future. The kingdom promises await consummation, not cancellation.

This matters greatly for the doctrine of the Second Coming. If Christ does not return, the full public vindication of the faithful remains unrealized. If Christ does not return, the promised defeat of beastly power remains incomplete. If Christ does not return, the Davidic kingship remains unfulfilled in its visible scope, the inheritance of the earth remains unrealized, and the restoration prophecies remain suspended. The return of Christ is therefore necessary, not only because the New Testament declares it, but because the Old Testament promises demand it.

The Prophets Require the Return of the King

The cumulative testimony of the Old Testament is clear. The Messiah would suffer, but He would also reign. He would be pierced, but He would also judge the nations. He would be cut off, but He would also receive everlasting dominion. He would come lowly, but He would also come in victory. The kingdom of God would not remain an invisible abstraction. It would break the power of rebellious kingdoms, vindicate the faithful, raise the dead, and fill the earth with righteousness and the knowledge of Jehovah.

The prophets therefore do not merely allow for the doctrine of the Second Coming. They require it. The first coming of Christ fulfilled the line of humiliation, suffering, and atonement. The second coming will fulfill the line of open kingship, final judgment, resurrection, and kingdom triumph. The Old Testament's hope is therefore not exhausted at Calvary or even at the ascension. It stretches forward to the day when the Son of Man comes with the clouds, when the beastly powers are judged, when the kingdom is openly established, and when the promises made to the faithful are brought to their appointed completion.

For that reason the Christian hope is not a departure from the Old Testament. It is its fulfillment. The coming King announced by the prophets is Jesus Christ. The same Messiah who suffered for sins will return to reign. The same Son of David who came in humility will come in glory. The same pierced One will be seen by every eye. The Old Testament foundations therefore stand firm beneath the doctrine of the Second Coming, and they direct all expectation toward the day when Jehovah's Anointed appears to judge, to reign, and to fulfill every promise made to His people.

Chapter 3 — Jesus' Own Teaching About His Return

The Lord's Own Testimony About the End

The doctrine of the Second Coming does not rest only on apostolic interpretation or prophetic anticipation. It rests on the direct teaching of Jesus Christ Himself. The Lord did not leave His disciples with a vague expectation that history would somehow improve or that His cause would slowly triumph without decisive intervention. He taught plainly that He would return. He warned of deception before that return. He described persecution, tribulation, and lawlessness preceding it. He spoke of His appearing in unmistakable glory. He connected that appearing with the gathering of His followers, the judgment of the wicked, and the close of the present age. For that reason, any faithful doctrine of the Second Coming must begin with the words of Jesus.

The fullest treatment of this subject appears in the Olivet Discourse, preserved in Matthew 24–25, Mark 13, and Luke 21. These chapters do not represent random sayings loosely gathered around prophetic themes. They form a coherent discourse given in response to specific questions from the disciples. As Jesus sat on the Mount of Olives overlooking Jerusalem and the temple, His disciples asked about the destruction of the temple, the sign of His presence, and the conclusion of the age (Matt. 24:1–3). The Lord's answer moves through near and far elements, but its dominant thrust is unmistakable: the people of God must not be deceived, must endure through increasing pressure, and must remain watchful until the visible appearing of the Son of Man.

Jesus' teaching therefore rejects two opposite errors. On the one hand, it rejects the idea that the return of Christ is a minor doctrine. The Lord devoted sustained instruction to it. On the other hand, it rejects sensationalism, because Jesus repeatedly warns His followers not to be led astray by false claims, premature excitement, or deceptive appearances (Matt. 24:4–5, 11, 23–26; Mark 13:5–6, 21–23; Luke 21:8). The true doctrine of Christ's return is neither indifference nor fanaticism. It is sober expectation governed by the words of Jesus.

The Questions That Framed the Discourse

The discourse begins with Jesus' shocking prediction that the temple would be so thoroughly judged that "not one stone here will be left upon another, which will not be torn down" (Matt. 24:2; Mark 13:2; Luke 21:6). The disciples then ask when these things will occur and what sign will mark the larger consummation. Matthew gives the fullest wording: "Tell us, when will these things happen, and what will be the sign of Your presence and of the conclusion of the age?" (Matt. 24:3). Mark and Luke preserve the same concern in slightly different form (Mark 13:4; Luke 21:7).

This question is important because it shows that Jesus' teaching is eschatological in structure. He is not merely giving general advice about suffering. He is answering questions about the progress of history toward its climactic end. The destruction of Jerusalem and the temple lies within the horizon of the discourse, but the discourse itself reaches beyond that event. Jesus moves from preliminary signs to intensifying distress, then to the abomination, unparalleled tribulation, cosmic disturbance, the appearing of the Son of Man, and the gathering of His chosen ones (Matt. 24:29–31; Mark 13:24–27; Luke 21:25–28). The shape of the answer therefore resists every reduction of the discourse to one local first-century crisis alone.

This is especially clear because Jesus draws directly from Daniel. He refers to "the abomination of desolation spoken of through Daniel the prophet" (Matt. 24:15; Mark 13:14). He uses the title "Son of Man" in connection with coming on the clouds, language rooted in Daniel 7:13–14. He describes a unique tribulation that echoes Daniel 12:1. Jesus is therefore not creating a new prophetic framework detached from earlier revelation. He is interpreting the time of the end through the Danielic structure already established in Scripture. His return belongs to that framework of final crisis, heavenly intervention, judgment, and kingdom triumph.

The First Warning: Deception

The first emphasis in the Olivet Discourse is not chronology but deception. Jesus begins, "See to it that no one misleads you. For many will come in My name, saying, 'I am the Christ,' and will mislead many" (Matt. 24:4–5). Mark records, "See to it that no one misleads you. Many will come in My name, saying, 'I am He!' and will mislead many" (Mark 13:5–6). Luke likewise says, "See to it that you are not misled; for many will come in My name, saying, 'I am He,' and, 'The time is at hand'; do not go after them" (Luke 21:8).

This opening warning governs the entire discourse. False christs, false prophets, and deceptive claims about the nearness or presence of the end are among the first signs that the people of God must resist. Jesus does not treat deception as a peripheral threat. He treats it as central. The reason is plain. Whenever believers are eager for the coming kingdom, they are vulnerable to those who promise secret knowledge, special timing, or visible manifestations detached from Scripture. That is why Christ begins with a command of vigilance.

The warning also reveals something about the nature of the true return. If false claims can arise, the real event must be of a kind that exposes them all as false. The counterfeit depends on ambiguity. The true appearing of Christ will not. Jesus later makes this explicit: "Therefore if they say to you, 'Look, He is in the wilderness,' do not go out, or, 'Look, He is in the inner rooms,' do not believe them" (Matt. 24:26). Secret messianic appearances are excluded by the Lord's own words. The true return of Christ is not private, hidden, or localized in some obscure place. It is public, universal, and unmistakable.

Edward D. Andrews

Wars, Tumults, and Preliminary Sorrows

After warning about deception, Jesus speaks of wars, rumors of wars, earthquakes, famines, pestilences, and disturbances among the nations (Matt. 24:6–8; Mark 13:7–8; Luke 21:9–11). Yet He is careful to say, "see that you are not frightened, for those things must take place, but that is not yet the end" (Matt. 24:6). Mark says, "Such things must take place; but that is not yet the end" (Mark 13:7). Luke says, "do not be terrified; for these things must take place first, but the end does not follow immediately" (Luke 21:9).

This is another crucial correction to prophetic sensationalism. Not every upheaval is the end. Not every war announces the final appearing of Christ. Not every earthquake or famine should be treated as if it settles the timetable. Jesus teaches that such things belong to the convulsions of the present age. Matthew calls them "the beginning of birth pains" (Matt. 24:8). Birth pains signal that something is coming, but they are not themselves the final event. The disciples therefore must not confuse preliminary sorrows with consummation.

The phrase "must take place" is also significant. Jesus is not describing random chaos. He is speaking of events that unfold within divine necessity. History is not autonomous. Even the turmoil of nations occurs under the sovereignty of Jehovah. Yet the Lord insists that the faithful interpret these things rightly. They are not to panic. They are to discern that the age is moving toward its appointed end, but they are not to equate every upheaval with the appearing itself.

Persecution, Hatred, and Apostasy

The discourse then moves from general upheaval to direct pressure upon the followers of Christ. Jesus says, "Then they will deliver you to tribulation, and will kill you, and you will be hated by all the nations because of My name" (Matt. 24:9). Mark speaks similarly of being handed over to courts, beaten in synagogues, and brought before governors and kings for His sake (Mark 13:9). Luke emphasizes betrayal by parents, brothers, relatives, and friends, and the hatred believers will experience because of His name (Luke 21:12–17).

These words show that the doctrine of Christ's return is inseparable from the doctrine of Christian endurance. Jesus does not prepare His disciples for an easy passage into glory. He prepares them for opposition. The church in the present age is not promised cultural dominance before Christ returns. It is promised conflict, witness, and perseverance. This does not mean every believer in every place experiences the same degree of suffering at all times, but it does mean that the kingdom of God advances in a world fundamentally hostile to the Messiah.

Jesus also warns that "many will fall away and will betray one another and hate one another" (Matt. 24:10). False prophets will arise and mislead many. "Because lawlessness is increased, most people's love will grow cold" (Matt. 24:11–12). Here the Lord goes beyond persecution from outside to corruption from within the professing sphere. Apostasy is part of the end-time environment. Outward attachment to the faith will not guarantee perseverance. False teaching and moral collapse will expose many whose profession is not rooted in true allegiance.

Yet Jesus immediately adds the promise, "the one who has endured to the end, he will be saved" (Matt. 24:13; Mark

13:13). Endurance is therefore not a marginal virtue. It is the hallmark of genuine discipleship under eschatological pressure. Salvation is not presented here as a static possession detached from perseverance. It is the inheritance of those who remain faithful through deception, hatred, and tribulation. This harmonizes perfectly with the wider New Testament pattern in which believers are called to steadfastness while awaiting the appearing of Christ (1 Thess. 1:10; 2 Tim. 4:8; Heb. 9:28; Jas. 5:7–8).

The Gospel of the Kingdom and the End

Jesus then states, "This gospel of the kingdom shall be preached in the whole inhabited earth for a witness to all the nations, and then the end will come" (Matt. 24:14). Mark places the same point in this form: "The gospel must first be preached to all the nations" (Mark 13:10). The good news is specifically called "the gospel of the kingdom." That is important. Jesus' return is not detached from the kingdom message. The One who comes is the King, and the gospel announces His rightful rule.

The preaching of the kingdom to all nations does not mean that every individual without exception must hear before Christ returns, nor does it imply that the world will be converted through human preaching before His coming. Rather, it means that the kingdom message will be proclaimed throughout the nations as a witness. The church exists in the last days as a witnessing people, testifying to the coming reign of Christ in the midst of a rebellious world. That witness continues until the end. The missionary task is therefore tied directly to eschatology. The kingdom must be announced before the King appears.

This also prevents prophetic passivity. Believers do not merely wait. They proclaim. The certainty of Christ's return does not diminish evangelism. It intensifies it. The church preaches because the world is moving toward judgment and because the kingdom of God will soon be manifested openly.

The Abomination and the Great Tribulation

The discourse then narrows into the concentrated crisis of the time of the end. "Therefore when you see the abomination of desolation which was spoken of through Daniel the prophet, standing in the holy place," Jesus says, "let the reader understand" (Matt. 24:15). Mark gives a similar form: "when you see the abomination of desolation standing where it should not be" (Mark 13:14). Luke expresses the same reality in more immediately historical terms: "when you see Jerusalem surrounded by armies, then recognize that her desolation is at hand" (Luke 21:20).

Jesus intentionally directs His disciples back to Daniel. The "abomination of desolation" belongs to the prophetic pattern of desecration, anti-God arrogance, and final crisis. Daniel's visions present both immediate historical patterns and an intensified end-time culmination in which opposition to God reaches a mature form (Dan. 8:9–14; 9:27; 11:31; 12:11). By invoking Daniel, Jesus makes clear that He is interpreting His own return within that same structure. The crisis before His appearing is not random. It is the culmination of a prophetic pattern already revealed.

The response Jesus commands is urgent. Those in Judea are to flee to the mountains. There must be no hesitation, no delay, no attempt to preserve possessions (Matt. 24:16–20; Mark 13:14–18; Luke 21:21–24). He then says, "for then there will be a great tribulation, such as has not occurred since the beginning of the world until now, nor ever will" (Matt. 24:21). Daniel 12:1 had already spoken of "a time of distress such as never occurred since there was a nation until that time." Jesus' language deliberately echoes that prophecy. The great tribulation is therefore not an ordinary period of hardship. It is the unparalleled end-time crisis preceding the visible return of the Son of Man.

This language also rules out attempts to flatten all tribulation in history into one undifferentiated category. Believers have always suffered, but Jesus speaks here of a unique intensification. That final tribulation belongs to the time of the end, not to every age equally. Yet even here Jesus gives a word of mercy: "unless those days had been cut short, no flesh would have been saved; but for the sake of the chosen ones those days will be cut short" (Matt. 24:22; Mark 13:20). The tribulation is severe, but it is measured. God remains sovereign. The days are not open-ended. They are cut short for the sake of the chosen ones.

The Visible and Unmistakable Return of the Son of Man

Immediately after warning about false claims of Christ's presence in hidden places, Jesus declares the true nature of His return: "For just as the lightning comes from the east and shines as far as the west, so will the presence of the Son of Man be" (Matt. 24:27). This statement is decisive. Lightning is not private. It is public, sudden, and impossible to conceal. Christ's return therefore cannot be a secret or invisible event known only to a select few. It is a cosmic manifestation.

Jesus intensifies this further: "Immediately after the tribulation of those days the sun will be darkened, and the moon will not give its light, and the stars will fall from heaven, and the powers of the heavens will be shaken" (Matt. 24:29; Mark 13:24–25; Luke 21:25–26). The language is apocalyptic and draws from Old Testament descriptions of divine judgment and world-shaking intervention (Isa. 13:10; Joel 2:10, 31; Hag. 2:6). The point is not that readers should indulge in uncontrolled symbolism, but that Jesus is describing the upheaval accompanying divine intervention. The present order is shaken because the King is appearing.

Then comes the key statement: "And then the sign of the Son of Man will appear in heaven, and then all the tribes of the earth will mourn, and they will see the Son of Man coming on the clouds of heaven with power and great glory" (Matt. 24:30). Mark says, "then they will see the Son of Man coming in clouds with great power and glory" (Mark 13:26). Luke says, "then they will see the Son of Man coming in a cloud with power and great glory" (Luke 21:27).

This language combines Daniel 7:13 with Zechariah 12:10–12. The One who comes is the Son of Man invested with heavenly authority. The tribes mourn because His appearing means judgment, exposure, and the end of rebellious autonomy. The return is visible. "They will see." It is glorious. It comes with "power and great glory." It is public. All the tribes of the earth are involved. Jesus therefore leaves no room for theories that reduce His return to an invisible heavenly transition or to a hidden event preceding a later public event. The coming He describes is the public event.

Luke adds a pastoral note: "when these things begin to take place, straighten up and lift up your heads, because your redemption is drawing near" (Luke 21:28). For the world, the return means terror and mourning. For the faithful, it means redemption drawing near. That contrast is central to

Edward D. Andrews

Jesus' teaching. The same event that judges the wicked delivers the righteous.

The Gathering of the Chosen Ones

Jesus immediately connects His appearing with the gathering of His followers. "And He will send forth His angels with a great trumpet and they will gather together His chosen ones from the four winds, from one end of the sky to the other" (Matt. 24:31). Mark says, "then He will send forth the angels, and will gather together His chosen ones from the four winds, from the farthest end of the earth to the farthest end of heaven" (Mark 13:27).

This gathering is not separate from the visible appearing. It follows it directly. The Son of Man appears, angels are sent, the trumpet sounds, and the chosen ones are gathered. This harmonizes with Paul's teaching in 1 Thessalonians 4:16–17, where the Lord descends, the dead in Christ are raised, and the living are gathered together with them. Jesus does not speak here in the language of a secret removal before tribulation. He speaks of a gathering that takes place in connection with His open and glorious return after the tribulation of those days.

The trumpet language is important because it signals divine assembly, intervention, and kingdom transition. It recalls Old Testament themes of gathering and restoration (Isa. 27:13) and anticipates apostolic teaching on resurrection and transformation (1 Cor. 15:52; 1 Thess. 4:16). Jesus' point is that His people will not be scattered forever under the pressure of the nations. When He appears, they will be gathered by divine authority.

This gathering also connects the doctrine of Christ's return to the doctrine of resurrection, even though Matthew 24 itself does not spell out the full resurrection sequence in the same detail as Paul. The wider New Testament makes clear that the gathering of Christ's people at His coming includes both the raising of the dead in Christ and the transformation of the living (1 Cor. 15:23, 51–52; 1 Thess. 4:16–17). Yet that resurrection hope must not be flattened into one undifferentiated reward. Scripture later distinguishes between the select holy ones who receive immortality for heavenly reign with Christ and the broader righteous who receive everlasting life under God's kingdom. Jesus' discourse therefore stands in full harmony with the fuller apostolic explanation.

The Days of Noah and the Suddenness of Judgment

Jesus then turns to the days of Noah as an analogy for the manner in which His coming overtakes the world (Matt. 24:37–39; Luke 17:26–30 also reflects the same teaching). People were eating, drinking, marrying, and being given in marriage until the flood came and swept them all away. The point is not that ordinary activities are sinful in themselves. The point is that the world continued in apparent normalcy, indifferent to divine warning, until judgment arrived suddenly.

"So will the presence of the Son of Man be" (Matt. 24:39). The coming of Christ will therefore divide humanity abruptly and decisively. Jesus says, "then there will be two men in the field; one will be taken and one will be left. Two women will be grinding at the mill; one will be taken and one will be left" (Matt. 24:40–41). The emphasis is not on an invisible disappearance, but on sudden separation in judgment and deliverance. The flood analogy controls the meaning. In Noah's day the ungodly were overtaken, while the righteous were preserved through God's intervention.

Jesus uses that pattern to warn His hearers of the decisiveness of His coming.

This is why the correct response is watchfulness. "Therefore keep on the watch, because you do not know which day your Lord is coming" (Matt. 24:42). Mark presses this theme repeatedly: "Be on guard! Keep awake! For you do not know when the appointed time will come" (Mark 13:33), and again, "what I say to you I say to all, 'Keep awake!'" (Mark 13:37). Luke similarly says believers must "keep on the watch at all times" (Luke 21:36). The uncertainty concerns timing, not certainty of the event itself. The Lord will return. The disciples do not know the exact day and hour. Therefore they must live in constant readiness.

Jesus Connected His Return With Judgment

The Olivet Discourse does not end in Matthew 24. It flows directly into the parables and scenes of Matthew 25, where Jesus expounds the moral and judicial implications of His return. The faithful and evil slave are contrasted, with the evil slave judged because he says in his heart, "My master is not coming for a long time" (Matt. 24:48–51). The ten virgins are divided between wise and foolish, and the door is shut upon those unprepared for the bridegroom's arrival (Matt. 25:1–13). The talents are distributed and later reviewed when the master returns, rewarding faithfulness and condemning slothful wickedness (Matt. 25:14–30).

These parables all reinforce the same doctrine. Christ's return brings accountability. It is not a mere spectacle. It is the day when hidden loyalties are exposed. Preparedness is not measured by prophetic excitement but by faithfulness, vigilance, and obedience.

The sheep and goats scene then brings the discourse to its climactic judicial form. "When the Son of Man comes in His glory, and all the angels with Him, then He will sit on His glorious throne" (Matt. 25:31). All the nations are gathered before Him, and He separates them as a shepherd separates sheep from goats (Matt. 25:32–33). The righteous inherit the kingdom prepared for them, while the wicked depart into punishment (Matt. 25:34, 41, 46). Here again, Jesus explicitly connects His coming with judgment of the nations and kingdom inheritance for the faithful. His return is not merely a moment of reunion. It is also the enthronement scene of the Judge.

This judicial emphasis appears elsewhere in Jesus' teaching as well. In Matthew 16:27 He says, "the Son of Man is going to come in the glory of His Father with His angels, and will then repay every man according to his deeds." In John 5:28–29 He declares that "an hour is coming, in which all who are in the tombs will hear His voice, and will come out; those who did the good deeds to a resurrection of life, those who committed the evil deeds to a resurrection of judgment." Jesus therefore links His return with universal accountability and with resurrection itself.

Jesus Connected His Return With Resurrection

Although the Olivet Discourse emphasizes the visible appearing, gathering, and judgment associated with Christ's return, Jesus' broader teaching also places resurrection at the center of the final hope. In John 6 He repeatedly says that He will raise up the faithful "on the last day" (John 6:39–40, 44, 54). In John 11, after Lazarus dies, Martha says, "I know that he will rise again in the resurrection on the last day" (John 11:24). Jesus does not correct her expectation of a future resurrection day. He deepens it by centering it in Himself: "I am the resurrection and the life" (John 11:25).

The same pattern appears in John 5:28–29, where all in the tombs hear His voice and come out. This is not the language of immortal souls continuing in conscious life independent of resurrection. It is the language of those in the tombs being called forth by the authority of the Son. Jesus' doctrine is therefore fully consistent with the biblical teaching that life beyond death depends on resurrection, not on the innate indestructibility of human nature.

When this is read together with Matthew 24:31 and the apostolic interpretation in 1 Corinthians 15 and 1 Thessalonians 4, the picture is coherent. Christ appears visibly. His people are gathered. The dead are raised. The living are transformed. The wicked are judged. The kingdom moves into its next revealed stage. But the life granted in that future order is not described in exactly the same way for all the saved. The heavenly co-rulers receive immortality, while the broader righteous receive everlasting life. Jesus' own teaching supplies the foundation, and the apostles later expand upon it without contradiction.

The Practical Force of Christ's Teaching

Jesus' teaching about His return is never given merely to satisfy curiosity. It is given to shape conduct. The dominant imperatives are clear: do not be deceived, do not be terrified, endure to the end, proclaim the gospel of the kingdom, flee when the appointed crisis comes, keep on the watch, be ready, remain faithful.

That pastoral force must not be lost. The doctrine of the Second Coming is not an excuse for speculation. It is a call to readiness. The Lord does not invite His disciples to obsess over hidden chronology. He commands them to remain loyal in the face of deception, persecution, delay, and lawlessness. The true test of eschatological faithfulness is not whether one can construct elaborate timelines. It is whether one remains obedient while awaiting the coming King.

This is why Jesus consistently joins warning with hope. He warns of deception because His disciples need truth. He warns of tribulation because they need endurance. He warns of judgment because they need sobriety. But He also promises that their redemption draws near, that the chosen ones will be gathered, that the kingdom will be inherited, and that the Son of Man will come in glory. The same Lord who predicts tribulation also guarantees triumph.

The Lord's Own Doctrine of His Return

The teaching of Jesus leaves no room for uncertainty about the basic contours of the doctrine. His return will follow a period marked by deception, upheaval, persecution, apostasy, and final tribulation. It will be visible, public, and unmistakable, like lightning flashing across the sky. It will occur with power, glory, angels, and trumpet. It will bring the gathering of His chosen ones. It will bring judgment upon the wicked. It will stand in continuity with Daniel's prophecy of the Son of Man, the abomination, the time of distress, and the kingdom.

The church therefore does not build its doctrine of the Second Coming by beginning with speculative systems and then fitting Jesus into them. It begins with the Lord's own words. Those words are clear enough to exclude secrecy, invisible coming theories, prophetic sensationalism, and moral indifference. They direct the faithful to watchfulness, endurance, proclamation, and hope. Above all, they direct attention to Jesus Christ Himself, the Son of Man who will come with power and great glory, gather His followers, judge the nations, and bring the present age to its appointed end under the sovereign purpose of Jehovah.

Chapter 4 — The Apostolic Doctrine of Christ's Return

The Apostolic Witness and the Hope of the Congregations

The apostles did not treat the return of Christ as an uncertain possibility or as a secondary theme standing at the edge of Christian doctrine. They proclaimed it as a certainty fixed in the purpose of God and central to the hope of the congregations. The risen Christ had ascended into heaven, but He had not withdrawn from history permanently. He would return personally, visibly, and gloriously to judge the world, raise the dead, gather His people, destroy the anti-God order, and bring His kingdom into its next decisive stage of manifestation. This was not private speculation among a few prophetic minds. It was the settled doctrine of the apostolic church.

The apostles wrote to congregations living under pressure, deception, grief, and opposition. Their answer was not to direct believers toward philosophical comfort, mystical interiority, or confidence in human progress. They directed them toward the return of Jesus Christ. Paul says that the Thessalonians had turned to God from idols "to wait for His Son from heaven" (1 Thess. 1:10). Peter says that believers are guarded through faith for a salvation ready to be revealed in the last time (1 Pet. 1:5). John says, "Beloved, now we are children of God, and it has not yet been made manifest what we will be. We know that whenever He is made manifest, we will be like Him" (1 John 3:2). Jude speaks of "waiting anxiously for the mercy of our Lord Jesus Christ to eternal life" (Jude 21). The church's posture was therefore forward-looking. It lived in remembrance of the cross and resurrection, but it also lived in expectation of the appearing of the Lord.

This expectation was not vague. The apostles did not merely say that Christ would somehow continue His influence. They taught that He would return personally. The angelic promise in Acts 1:11 remained foundational: "This Jesus who has been taken up from you into heaven will come in just the same way as you have watched Him go into heaven." Paul, Peter, John, and Jude all build on that same certainty. Their doctrine of the future is not abstract. It is Christ-centered, resurrection-centered, judgment-centered, and kingdom-centered.

Paul and the Return of Christ as the Church's Blessed Hope

Among the apostles, Paul gives the fullest doctrinal development of Christ's return in relation to resurrection, judgment, apostasy, and the kingdom. His teaching is not fragmented. It is coherent and ordered. He expects one visible return of Christ, not multiple disconnected phases. He connects that return with the resurrection of believers, the transformation of the living, the destruction of the lawless one, the day of the Lord, and the defeat of death itself.

This is clear from the beginning of his letters. In 1 Thessalonians 1:10, believers are described as those who "wait for His Son from heaven." In 1 Corinthians 1:7, the congregation is said to be "eagerly waiting for the revelation of our Lord Jesus Christ." In Philippians 3:20–21, Paul writes, "our citizenship exists in the heavens, from which also we eagerly wait for a Savior, the Lord Jesus Christ, who will transform our lowly body to be like His glorious body." The future orientation of apostolic faith is everywhere present. Christ is not merely the object of past faith. He is the object of future expectation.

Paul also ties Christian endurance directly to that future hope. In Titus 2:13 he calls believers to live soberly and righteously while "awaiting our blessed hope, the appearing of the glory of our great God and Savior Jesus Christ." In 2 Timothy 4:8 he speaks of the crown of righteousness that will be awarded "on that day" not only to him, but "to all those who have loved His appearing." The true Christian life therefore includes longing for Christ's appearing. A faith that has no place for the Lord's return has departed from the shape of apostolic Christianity.

First Thessalonians and the Comfort of Resurrection Hope

Paul's first letter to the Thessalonians is one of the clearest statements of the apostolic doctrine of Christ's return. The congregation was grieving over those who had

Edward D. Andrews

died, and Paul answers that grief by directing them to resurrection at Christ's coming. "We do not want you to be uninformed, brothers, about those who are asleep," he says, "so that you will not grieve as do the rest who have no hope" (1 Thess. 4:13). The metaphor of sleep here is not ornamental. It reflects the biblical understanding of death as the cessation of conscious life while awaiting resurrection. Paul does not comfort the believers by saying that the dead are already consciously reigning or enjoying immortal life apart from resurrection. His comfort is future-oriented. The dead in Christ will rise.

He explains the sequence plainly: "For the Lord Himself will descend from heaven with a shout, with the voice of an archangel and with the trumpet of God, and the dead in Christ will rise first. Then we who are alive, who remain, will be caught up together with them in clouds to meet the Lord in the air; and so we will always be with the Lord" (1 Thess. 4:16–17). Every element of the passage emphasizes publicity and divine intervention. The Lord Himself descends. There is a commanding shout. There is the voice of an archangel. There is the trumpet of God. Nothing in the passage suggests secrecy, invisibility, or a quiet spiritual transaction. Paul is describing the one great return of Christ in visible, historical power.

The order also matters. The dead in Christ rise first. Then the living are gathered together with them. This shows that resurrection is not peripheral to Paul's teaching. It is central. The dead do not bypass resurrection because of an immortal soul already enjoying full life elsewhere. Their hope is resurrection at Christ's coming. The living are not gathered in a separate earlier phase. They are transformed and gathered in the same climactic event. Paul's words leave no room for a secret removal of the church prior to the open appearing of Christ.

The purpose of this teaching is pastoral as much as doctrinal. "Therefore comfort one another with these words" (1 Thess. 4:18). The comfort is not abstract survival after death. It is the future reversal of death through resurrection. That is why 1 Thessalonians stands in perfect harmony with 1 Corinthians 15. The Christian hope is not innate immortality. It is the return of Christ and the resurrection of the dead.

The Day of the Lord in First Thessalonians

Paul continues immediately into the subject of the day of the Lord in 1 Thessalonians 5. "You yourselves know full well that the day of the Lord comes like a thief in the night" (1 Thess. 5:2). The point is not invisibility, but suddenness. For the unbelieving world, the day arrives unexpectedly. "When they are saying, 'Peace and safety,' then destruction will come upon them suddenly" (1 Thess. 5:3). The day of the Lord is therefore a day of judgment. It is not a vague spiritual era or a merely inward awakening. It is God's climactic intervention in history through Christ.

At the same time, Paul says believers are "not in darkness, that the day would overtake you like a thief" (1 Thess. 5:4). The faithful are not surprised because they are living in readiness. They are "sons of light and sons of day" and must therefore remain awake, sober, armed with faith, love, and the hope of salvation (1 Thess. 5:5–8). Apostolic eschatology is always ethical. The certainty of Christ's return calls for watchfulness, not date-setting; holiness, not sensationalism; readiness, not panic.

Edward D. Andrews

Second Thessalonians and the Events That Must Precede the Return

If 1 Thessalonians emphasizes comfort and hope, 2 Thessalonians adds doctrinal clarification. Some in the congregation had become unsettled by claims that the day of the Lord had already come. Paul corrects them with remarkable precision. "Now we ask you, brothers, concerning the coming of our Lord Jesus Christ and our gathering together to Him," he writes, "that you not be quickly shaken" (2 Thess. 2:1–2). The "coming" of Christ and the "gathering together" of believers are treated as parts of the same future event.

Paul then says, "Let no one deceive you in any way, because it will not come unless the apostasy comes first, and the man of lawlessness is revealed" (2 Thess. 2:3). This statement is decisive. The return of Christ is not presented as signless in the sense that nothing precedes it. Before the gathering of believers to Christ, there must be a great apostasy and the unveiling of the man of lawlessness. The apostolic doctrine therefore rejects every theology that requires a secret, any-moment removal of believers before the final rebellion matures. Paul explicitly says certain identifiable events must come first.

The man of lawlessness is then described as one who "opposes and exalts himself above every so-called god or object of worship" and who displays himself in the temple of God (2 Thess. 2:4). Whether this is understood as an individual concentration of rebellion or as an institutionalized apostate order, the point is clear: before Christ returns, there will be a mature and blasphemous anti-God rebellion arising in connection with the professing sphere of religion.

Paul then declares the outcome: "Then that lawless one will be revealed, whom the Lord Jesus will slay with the breath of His mouth and bring to nothing by the appearance of His coming" (2 Thess. 2:8). The lawless one is not overcome by gradual reform, religious revival, or human politics. He is destroyed by the appearing of Christ's coming. This destruction is public and decisive. The phrase "appearance of His coming" underscores the visible majesty of the event. It is the opposite of a hidden or secret coming.

Thus the sequence in 2 Thessalonians is clear: apostasy, revelation of lawlessness, coming of Christ, destruction of the lawless order. Paul's doctrine is therefore sequential, visible, and historical. Christ's return ends the rebellion and inaugurates the next stage of kingdom administration. Evil is not left to fade slowly into irrelevance. It is judged by the appearing of the Lord.

First Corinthians 15 and the Resurrection at Christ's Coming

Paul's fullest treatment of resurrection appears in 1 Corinthians 15, and it is impossible to understand the apostolic doctrine of Christ's return without it. The chapter is structured around the resurrection of Christ as the guarantee of the future resurrection of those who belong to Him. "But now Christ has been raised from the dead, the firstfruits of those who have fallen asleep" (1 Cor. 15:20). The term "firstfruits" indicates both priority and guarantee. Christ's resurrection is the first stage of a harvest that must continue.

Paul then sets out the order: "each in his own order: Christ the firstfruits, afterward those who are Christ's at His coming" (1 Cor. 15:23). This is crucial. Those who belong to Christ are raised at His coming, not at the moment of death. The apostolic hope is tied to the Parousia, the return of Christ. Resurrection is not postponed indefinitely, but neither is it detached from the appearing of the Lord. It belongs to that event.

Paul continues: "then comes the end, when He hands over the kingdom to the God and Father, when He has abolished all rule and all authority and power. For He must reign until He has put all His enemies under His feet. The last enemy that will be abolished is death" (1 Cor. 15:24–26). Here resurrection, kingdom, and the defeat of death are inseparably joined. Christ's return is not merely the close of one chapter. It is the decisive stage in the destruction of enemies, culminating in the abolition of death itself. This again shows that the apostles did not separate eschatology into disconnected doctrines. Resurrection, judgment, reign, and final victory belong together.

The chapter later addresses the transformation of the living. "We will not all sleep, but we will all be changed, in a moment, in the twinkling of an eye, at the last trumpet" (1 Cor. 15:51–52). The dead are raised imperishable, and the living are transformed. This change occurs "at the last trumpet," not in some invisible preliminary event. The trumpet again signals public divine intervention. Paul says, "this mortal must put on immortality" (1 Cor. 15:53). Yet that language must be handled carefully. Immortality is not a natural human possession, nor is it spoken of in Scripture as the universal reward of all the righteous. It is the indestructible life granted in connection with the heavenly calling and reign of Christ's co-rulers, whereas the broader righteous receive eternal life under God's kingdom. The whole chapter therefore stands against every doctrine of an immortal soul existing independently of resurrection and against the idea that all future life is described in exactly the same terms.

Peter and the Day of the Lord

Peter's teaching agrees fully with Paul's. In 2 Peter 3 he warns that scoffers will come, saying, "Where is the promise of His coming?" (2 Pet. 3:4). Their error lies not merely in doubting chronology but in denying the certainty of divine intervention. Peter answers by recalling the flood as a past act of judgment and then declaring that the present heavens and earth are reserved for fire "for the day of judgment and destruction of ungodly men" (2 Pet. 3:7).

He then says, "the day of the Lord will come like a thief, in which the heavens will pass away with a roar and the elements will be destroyed with intense heat" (2 Pet. 3:10). Like Paul, Peter emphasizes suddenness for the ungodly, not invisibility. The day is public and catastrophic in effect. It is a day of judgment. Yet Peter's purpose is pastoral: "since all these things are to be destroyed in this way, what sort of people ought you to be in holy conduct and godliness" (2 Pet. 3:11). The doctrine of Christ's return is therefore moral in force. It is meant to produce holiness, not idle speculation.

Peter also directs hope toward the future order of righteousness: "according to His promise we are looking for new heavens and a new earth, in which righteousness dwells" (2 Pet. 3:13). The apostolic doctrine does not end with destruction. Judgment clears the way for restoration under God's reign. That is why believers wait in hope rather than fear.

John and the Manifestation of Christ

John's witness is equally clear. In Revelation 1:7 he declares, "Look, He is coming with the clouds, and every eye will see Him." This is not secret or symbolic in a way that empties the event of historical reality. It is public manifestation. The tribes of the earth mourn because the appearing of Christ means accountability and judgment.

In 1 John 3:2–3, John links Christ's appearing to transformation and holiness: "we know that whenever He is made manifest, we will be like Him, because we will see Him just as He is. And everyone who has this hope fixed on Him purifies himself just as that one is pure." The apostolic logic is powerful. The future manifestation of Christ produces present purification. The doctrine is not given to encourage abstraction. It shapes the life of obedience.

Revelation also presents Christ's return as the moment of decisive victory over rebellious power. He appears as the rider on the white horse, judging and waging war in righteousness (Rev. 19:11–16). The beastly order is overthrown, the false prophet is judged, and the way is opened for the millennial reign described in Revelation 20. John therefore confirms the same broad pattern seen in Paul: visible return, judgment of evil, and kingdom administration following that victory.

Jude and the Return in Judgment

Jude, though brief, also bears direct witness to Christ's future coming in judgment. He cites the ancient prophecy: "Look, the Lord came with many thousands of His holy ones, to execute judgment upon all" (Jude 14–15). The point is unmistakable. The Lord comes as Judge. The ungodly are exposed and condemned for their ungodly deeds and harsh words. Jude's concern throughout the letter is false teachers, corruption, and apostasy, and he answers these threats not with denial of judgment but with certainty that the Lord will come.

He then exhorts believers to keep themselves in God's love, "waiting anxiously for the mercy of our Lord Jesus Christ to eternal life" (Jude 21). Mercy and judgment meet at the return of Christ. For the ungodly, His coming means exposure and ruin. For the faithful, it means mercy unto life. Jude therefore stands in full harmony with the wider apostolic witness.

The Apostolic Doctrine as One Coherent Hope

When the teaching of Paul, Peter, John, and Jude is brought together, the apostolic doctrine of Christ's return is strikingly unified. Christ will return personally. His coming will be visible and public. It will not be secret, invisible, or merely spiritual. It will occur after the maturation of rebellion and apostasy, not before all prophetic signs. It will bring resurrection of the dead, transformation of the living, judgment of the wicked, destruction of the lawless and beastly order, and the open advance of Christ's kingdom.

This doctrine is also inseparable from the biblical teaching on death and resurrection. The apostles do not comfort believers with the idea that death is the release of an immortal soul into conscious heavenly bliss. They comfort believers with resurrection at Christ's return. The dead sleep until awakened by the voice of the Lord. Christ the firstfruits guarantees that those who belong to Him will be raised at His coming. Death remains an enemy until it is finally abolished. But the apostolic teaching does not apply immortality indiscriminately to every saved person. Immortality is the gift of indestructible life granted to the select resurrected holy ones who reign with Christ, whereas eternal life is the unending life granted to the broader righteous according to God's kingdom purpose.

The apostolic doctrine is finally pastoral in purpose. It calls the church to watchfulness, holiness, courage, endurance, and faithful witness. Believers are to love His appearing, not speculate recklessly about timing. They are to be comforted in grief, not by Greek ideas of disembodied survival, but by the certainty of resurrection. They are to resist deception and apostasy because the coming Lord will judge all falsehood. They are to persevere in faith because the appearing of Christ will vindicate the faithful and bring the present age to its appointed end.

The apostles therefore hand down no uncertain message. Jesus Christ will return. He will come personally, visibly, and gloriously. He will raise the dead, transform the living, judge the world, destroy the anti-God order, and establish His righteous rule. In that future order, the life granted by God is not described in one undifferentiated way for all the saved: the heavenly co-rulers receive immortality, while the broader righteous receive eternal life. This is the apostolic doctrine of Christ's return, and it remains the church's living hope until the day the Lord Himself descends from heaven and all His words are fulfilled.

Chapter 5 — The Man of Lawlessness and the Final Apostasy

The Apostolic Warning About the Rebellion Before the End

The return of Jesus Christ does not occur in a theological vacuum. The New Testament repeatedly teaches that before His appearing there will be a mature expression of anti-God rebellion, marked by deception, apostasy, false worship, and lawlessness. Jesus warned of false christs, false prophets, and increasing lawlessness before the coming of the Son of Man (Matt. 24:4–5, 11–12, 23–27). John warned that many antichrists had already arisen and that the spirit of antichrist was already in the world (1 John 2:18, 22; 4:1–3; 2 John 7). Paul warned of a coming apostasy and the

69

revelation of "the man of lawlessness" before the return of Christ (2 Thess. 2:1–8). Revelation unveils the mature anti-God order under the dragon, the beast, the false prophet, the image, and the mark of the beast (Rev. 12:17; 13:1–18; 19:19–20). These passages describe one broad conflict, but they do not use their terms carelessly, nor do they invite the interpreter to flatten every prophetic enemy into one simplistic figure.

The clearest apostolic treatment of the final apostasy appears in 2 Thessalonians 2. Some in Thessalonica had apparently been shaken by claims that the day of the Lord had already arrived (2 Thess. 2:1–2). Paul therefore writes, not to stir prophetic excitement, but to restore theological steadiness. He reminds the congregation that certain events must occur before the coming of Christ and the gathering of believers to Him. The apostasy must come first. The man of lawlessness must be revealed. The restraining influence must be removed. The lawless one will then operate in satanic deception until he is destroyed by the appearance of Christ's coming (2 Thess. 2:3–8). This sequence is vital. The return of Christ is certain, but the church must understand that the path to that return includes a concentrated outbreak of rebellion against God.

The Apostasy Must Come First

Paul writes, "Let no one deceive you in any way, because it will not come unless the apostasy comes first, and the man of lawlessness is revealed" (2 Thess. 2:3). The term translated "apostasy" refers to rebellion, falling away, or defection. In this context it is not mere social decline, political instability, or generic immorality. It is religious revolt. It is departure from revealed truth. Paul is describing something far more serious than the ordinary unbelief of the pagan world. He is describing rebellion connected with the visible sphere of profession, the very area where the truth of God had been confessed and known.

This fits the broader New Testament pattern. Jesus warned that many would fall away, betray one another, and be led astray by false prophets (Matt. 24:10–11). He taught that lawlessness would multiply and the love of many would grow cold (Matt. 24:12). Paul warned the Ephesian elders that savage wolves would arise from among the flock, speaking twisted things to draw disciples after themselves (Acts 20:29–30). He later told Timothy that in later times some would fall away from the faith, paying attention to deceitful spirits and teachings of demons (1 Tim. 4:1). Peter spoke of false teachers arising among the people and secretly introducing destructive heresies (2 Pet. 2:1). Jude warned of ungodly men who had crept in unnoticed, turning the grace of God into licentiousness and denying the Master (Jude 4). The apostasy in 2 Thessalonians 2 therefore belongs to a well-established apostolic theme: the danger is not only from hostile unbelief outside the visible sphere of religion, but from rebellion and corruption arising within it.

This must be stressed because it clarifies the nature of the final crisis. The last rebellion is not merely the rage of secular states against religion. It includes a religious dimension, a profaning corruption within the sphere that claims relation to God. The apostasy is thus doctrinal and worshipful before it is merely political. It is a falling away from truth, a defection from what God has revealed in Christ. This is why Paul frames it as something believers must know before the day of the Lord arrives. The church must not imagine that history moves straight from ordinary church life to the visible return of Christ without an intensified exposure of falsehood and revolt.

The Man of Lawlessness Revealed

Paul does not stop with the apostasy in general. He moves to its concentrated expression: "the man of lawlessness" (2 Thess. 2:3). This title is not casual. Lawlessness in Scripture is not merely lack of social restraint. It is rebellion against God's rule. It is the refusal of divine authority, the rejection of God's standard, and the self-assertion of man against his Creator. To call this figure or order the "man of lawlessness" is to identify it as the matured embodiment of anti-God rebellion.

Paul adds another designation in some manuscripts and translations: "the son of destruction" or "son of perdition" (2 Thess. 2:3). This expression indicates a being marked out by ruin, characterized by destruction, and destined for judgment. The title does not glorify the lawless one. It unmasks him. However exalted he may appear in the eyes of men, he is headed toward divine destruction.

The phrase "man of lawlessness" should not be handled simplistically. Paul does not say everything that might be said about the figure, nor does he reduce all prophetic opposition to this one term. He gives a focused description in his own categories. This is why the interpreter must resist careless synonym-making. John uses the word antichrist in a definitional, christological way for those who deny the truth about Jesus Christ, the Father, and the Son (1 John 2:22–23; 4:2–3; 2 John 7). Paul speaks of the man of lawlessness as the concentrated expression of apostate rebellion exalting itself in the sphere of worship (2 Thess. 2:3–4). Revelation portrays the beastly order, the false prophet, and the anti-God political-religious system demanding allegiance from the world (Rev. 13:1–18). These realities are related, but they are not identical in a careless one-to-one sense.

The man of lawlessness, then, is best understood as the mature public embodiment of anti-God rebellion arising out of apostasy and reaching a climactic expression before the return of Christ. Whether one emphasizes an individual focal point, an institutionalized order concentrated in one head, or both together, Paul's concern is theological rather than speculative. He is describing a real and final expression of lawless rebellion, not inviting endless guesses about passing political personalities.

Exalting Himself in the Sphere of Worship

Paul's description becomes even more pointed: the lawless one "opposes and exalts himself above every so-called god or object of worship, so that he takes his seat in the temple of God, publicly showing himself to be a god" (2 Thess. 2:4). This language reveals the fundamentally religious character of the rebellion. The lawless one is not merely a tyrant among tyrants. He is a profaning, self-exalting power in the realm of worship. He intrudes into the place that belongs to God and claims what belongs to God alone.

This language echoes Old Testament and Jewish apocalyptic patterns of arrogant rulers and desecrating powers. Daniel speaks repeatedly of kings who magnify themselves, speak monstrous things, exalt themselves above every god, and profane what is holy (Dan. 7:8, 20, 25; 8:11–12, 25; 11:36–39). The little horn wages war against the holy ones and exalts itself against heaven (Dan. 7:21, 25; 8:10–11). The king of Daniel 11 "will exalt himself and magnify himself above every god" (Dan. 11:36). Paul's language stands in continuity with these Danielic patterns. The man of lawlessness belongs to the same prophetic line of arrogant, desecrating rebellion, but Paul presents the final form of it in direct relation to the coming of Christ.

The phrase "temple of God" must also be treated carefully. Paul's wider usage often applies temple language to the people of God in their covenantal identity rather than to a standing physical structure alone (1 Cor. 3:16–17; 2 Cor. 6:16; Eph. 2:21). The immediate point in 2 Thessalonians 2 is not architectural curiosity. It is the sphere of worship and divine claim. The lawless one installs himself in the place belonging to God, in the realm where God is to be honored, and demands what belongs to God alone. This confirms once more that the final rebellion is not merely civil or military. It is religiously blasphemous. It is anti-God worship in concentrated form.

That description also keeps the church from a shallow reading of the end. The final crisis is not first about economics, geopolitical shifts, or public spectacle, though such things may be involved. It is about worship, allegiance, and truth. The lawless one opposes God not merely by violence, but by usurpation. He seeks to occupy the place of the Holy One. He is therefore not simply irreligious. He is pseudo-religious, anti-God, and self-deifying.

The Mystery of Lawlessness Already at Work

Paul then introduces a vital tension between present operation and future revelation: "the mystery of lawlessness is already at work" (2 Thess. 2:7). This statement mirrors John's teaching that many antichrists had already arisen and that the spirit of antichrist was already in the world (1 John 2:18; 4:3). The final lawless rebellion is not utterly disconnected from the present. Its principle is already active in history before its full unveiling.

The term "mystery" does not mean something irrational or unknowable. In Paul's usage, it refers to a reality once hidden but now revealed or unfolding under God's decree. The "mystery of lawlessness" therefore denotes the concealed but operative power of anti-God rebellion already working beneath the surface. The lawless principle is active in false teaching, apostasy, spiritual deception, and rebellion against divine truth. What is already operative in partial and hidden form will later be openly revealed in concentrated maturity.

This has immense pastoral importance. The church must not think only in terms of one future outbreak while ignoring present doctrinal revolt. The final lawless one is future in unveiling, but lawlessness is present in principle. The anti-God order is already moving toward its appointed climax. This is why discernment is needed now. False teaching about Christ, apostate religion, counterfeit spirituality, and self-exalting religious power are not harmless deviations. They belong to the same broad lawless movement that will culminate before the Lord returns.

Paul's language also guards against another error: the idea that the church can identify every present false teacher or oppressive ruler as the final man of lawlessness. The principle is already at work, but the final unveiling remains future. The present and future must both be maintained. There is already operation, but there will also be revelation. The church therefore lives in vigilance, recognizing the pattern without prematurely declaring every manifestation to be the final climax.

Edward D. Andrews

The Restrainer and the Timing of Revelation

Paul continues by explaining that the lawless one is not revealed immediately because something restrains him: "only he who now restrains will do so until he is taken out of the way" (2 Thess. 2:7). The precise identity of the restrainer has been debated through the centuries, and Paul himself does not define it in this passage. He had evidently instructed the Thessalonians orally about the matter (2 Thess. 2:5–6), but the letter gives no detailed exposition sufficient to produce dogmatic certainty.

That limitation must be respected. The passage clearly teaches restraint, but it does not authorize reckless certainty regarding the restrainer's exact identity. What matters most for Paul's argument is not speculative identification but theological function. The revelation of the lawless one occurs only at God's appointed time. Lawlessness is active, but it is restrained. The final outbreak of rebellion is neither autonomous nor outside divine control. It cannot emerge before the appointed moment. The restraining influence, whatever its precise form, serves the sovereign timing of God.

This reinforces a major biblical theme. Satanic and anti-God powers are real, deceptive, and dangerous, but they are never ultimate. They move only within divinely permitted limits. Job's adversary could not exceed the boundaries set by God (Job 1:12; 2:6). The dragon in Revelation acts only within the permissions and periods granted in the divine program (Rev. 13:5–7). The same is true here. The man of lawlessness is not free to emerge at will. He is restrained until the appointed time. The people of God therefore face real danger, but not ungoverned danger. History remains under Jehovah's rule.

The Coming of the Lawless One According to Satan

When the restraint is removed and the lawless one is revealed, Paul says his coming is "according to the working of Satan, with all power and signs and lying wonders" (2 Thess. 2:9). This is crucial for understanding the nature of the final rebellion. The lawless one is not merely a political opportunist or charismatic reformer. His activity is satanic in source and deceptive in effect. He comes with counterfeit power, deceptive signs, and false wonders.

This language again parallels Jesus' teaching. In the Olivet Discourse, Jesus warned that false christs and false prophets would arise and show great signs and wonders so as to mislead, if possible, even the chosen ones (Matt. 24:24; Mark 13:22). Revelation likewise presents the beast from the earth, later called the false prophet, as performing signs that deceive those who dwell on the earth and direct them into beast-worship (Rev. 13:11–14; 19:20). Paul's teaching therefore belongs within a larger biblical pattern: the final rebellion is marked by satanic deception, false signs, and counterfeit religion.

The expression "lying wonders" does not necessarily mean that every sign is a mere illusion with no real effect. It means the wonders serve falsehood. They are deceptive in source, message, and purpose. They do not lead men to the truth of God. They support rebellion, exalt the lawless order, and seduce those who do not love the truth. The issue is not raw power. The issue is allegiance. Satan can energize deceiving signs, but only to advance false worship and rebellion against God.

This keeps the church from naive fascination with the miraculous. Scripture never teaches that displays of power automatically validate truth. Signs must be judged by doctrine, by allegiance, and by fidelity to God's revelation. The lawless one comes in the power of Satan, not in the power of Jehovah. Whatever wonders attend him, they are instruments of delusion.

Those Who Perish Because They Did Not Love the Truth

Paul then explains why the deception succeeds: it comes "with every unrighteous deception among those who are perishing, because they did not receive the love of the truth so as to be saved" (2 Thess. 2:10). This statement is profound. The final deception is not merely an intellectual failure. It is a moral refusal. Men perish not because the truth was too obscure, but because they did not love it. Their judgment is bound up with their disposition toward divine revelation.

This is fully consistent with the rest of Scripture. Jesus said that men loved darkness rather than light because their deeds were evil (John 3:19–20). He said that those who are of God hear the words of God, but His opponents did not hear because they were not of God (John 8:47). The antichrist in John's letters is defined by denial of the truth about Jesus Christ (1 John 2:22–23; 4:2–3). Revelation depicts the beastly order as requiring allegiance from those whose names are not written in the Lamb's book of life (Rev. 13:8). The final rebellion therefore exposes what has been present all along: men do not merely lack information. They reject truth because they prefer unrighteousness.

Paul pushes further: "for this reason God sends upon them a deluding influence so that they will believe the lie, in order that they all may be judged who did not believe the truth, but took pleasure in unrighteousness" (2 Thess. 2:11–

THE SECOND COMING OF CHRIST

12). This is judicial language. God's action is not arbitrary. It is judgment upon those who have already rejected the truth. The lie becomes their judgment because they have refused the truth and delighted in unrighteousness.

This does not excuse their rebellion. It confirms its guilt. The lawless one deceives, Satan energizes, but men are judged because they did not believe the truth. The final apostasy is therefore both satanic and judicial. Satan deceives, but God hands over the truth-haters to the delusion they prefer. This is a sober warning. The rejection of truth is never harmless. Persistent refusal hardens the soul and prepares it for judgment.

Antichrist, Lawlessness, and the Final Rebellion

At this point the relationship between antichrist, apostasy, and the man of lawlessness must be stated carefully. The New Testament does not treat these terms as interchangeable labels for every enemy of God. John alone uses the word antichrist, and he defines it theologically: antichrist denies that Jesus is the Christ, denies the Father and the Son, and refuses to confess Jesus Christ as having come in the flesh (1 John 2:18–23; 4:2–3; 2 John 7). Antichrist is therefore fundamentally a christological and doctrinal category. It is already present in many deceivers, and it may also move toward a concentrated final expression.

Paul, however, uses different language. The "man of lawlessness" is the mature public embodiment of apostate rebellion exalting itself in the sphere of worship (2 Thess. 2:3–4). His concern is not to redefine John's term, but to present the final anti-God uprising in his own inspired categories. The lawless one stands in continuity with the antichristic principle because both are anti-Christ and anti-God, but Paul's emphasis falls on apostasy, self-exaltation, false worship, and final destruction at Christ's coming.

Revelation then adds further dimensions. The beast from the sea represents the final beastly political-religious order empowered by the dragon (Rev. 13:1–10). The beast from the earth, later called the false prophet, serves as the deceptive religious propagandist who directs men to worship the beast and receive his mark (Rev. 13:11–18; 19:20). Babylon the Great represents the corrupt world-order in its luxurious, idolatrous, and persecuting form (Rev. 17–18). These are all related manifestations within the final anti-God system, but the book does not collapse them into one featureless enemy. Nor should the interpreter.

Thus the relationship may be stated in this way: antichrist names the doctrinal and spiritual denial of Christ already at work in many deceivers; apostasy names the falling away from truth within the sphere of profession; the man of lawlessness names the concentrated mature expression of lawless self-exaltation before the return of Christ; the beastly order names the final anti-God political-religious system that demands allegiance from the world. These belong to one broad anti-God conflict energized by Satan, but the distinctions must be preserved if the biblical witness is to remain clear.

The Destruction of the Lawless One at Christ's Appearing

Paul's teaching does not leave the church staring endlessly at the rise of rebellion. It directs the eye to Christ's triumph. "Then that lawless one will be revealed, whom the Lord Jesus will slay with the breath of His mouth and bring to nothing by the appearance of His coming" (2 Thess. 2:8).

The final word does not belong to the apostasy, the lawless one, or the deluded world. It belongs to Jesus Christ.

The imagery of the "breath of His mouth" recalls Isaiah 11:4, where the Messiah strikes the earth with the rod of His mouth and slays the wicked with the breath of His lips. It is judicial and sovereign language. Christ does not struggle against the lawless one as though the outcome were uncertain. He destroys him by His appearing. The anti-God order reaches its mature expression, but it is crushed by the public manifestation of the Lord.

This is fully consistent with the rest of New Testament eschatology. Jesus said that after the tribulation of those days the Son of Man would appear in power and glory (Matt. 24:29–31). Revelation 19 presents the rider on the white horse coming in righteousness to judge and wage war, overthrowing the beast and the false prophet (Rev. 19:11–21). The lawless one, the beastly order, and the final rebellion are therefore not permanent mysteries but temporary eruptions judged by the returning King.

This is why Paul's doctrine is fundamentally pastoral. He writes to steady believers, not to terrify them. The apostasy must come. The lawless one must be revealed. Deception will intensify. But Christ will appear. The final rebellion is real, but it is doomed. The church must not be naive, but neither must it be afraid as though evil were ultimate. The lawless one is already marked for destruction.

The Church's Duty in the Face of Final Apostasy

Paul closes the section in 2 Thessalonians 2 by turning from prophecy to perseverance. Believers are beloved by the Lord, chosen for salvation through sanctification by the Spirit and faith in the truth, and called through the gospel to obtain the glory of Christ (2 Thess. 2:13–14). Therefore, he says, "stand firm and hold to the traditions which you

81

were taught" (2 Thess. 2:15). This is the practical force of the whole passage. The doctrine of the final apostasy is not given so that believers will become absorbed in prophetic speculation. It is given so that they will stand firm in the truth.

That remains the church's duty. The people of God must love the truth, not merely know facts about prophecy. They must resist false doctrine about Christ. They must discern apostate religion and lawless self-exaltation wherever it appears in principle. They must understand that final rebellion will mature before Christ returns. They must refuse every anti-God claim in the sphere of worship and conscience. Above all, they must remain steadfast in the apostolic gospel, knowing that the appearing of Christ will destroy the whole lawless and antichristic order.

The apostolic warning is therefore both severe and hopeful. Before the return of Christ, there will be a final and mature expression of anti-God rebellion. The apostasy will come. The man of lawlessness will be revealed. Satanic deception will intensify. But the lawless one will not endure. Jesus Christ will appear, and by the brightness of His coming He will bring the rebellion to nothing. The church waits, therefore, not in confusion, but in truth; not in panic, but in steadfastness; not in fear of the lawless one, but in hope of the King whose appearing ends all rebellion forever.

Chapter 6 — The Beastly Order and the Final Conflict

The Beastly Conflict in the Apocalypse

The book of Revelation presents the final conflict between the kingdom of God and the anti-God order in symbols that are theological, historical, and morally exact. These symbols are not given to stimulate panic or to encourage endless speculation about passing technologies, current personalities, or every new political crisis. They are given to unveil the character of the final rebellion, the nature of satanic deception, and the certainty of Christ's triumph. The focus of Revelation 12–13 is not curiosity but allegiance. The question is not merely who governs economically or militarily. The question is who receives worship, obedience, and loyalty. That is why the dragon, the beast from the sea, the beast from the earth, the image of the beast, and the mark of the beast must all be interpreted within the larger biblical conflict over truth, worship, and rule (Rev. 12:17; 13:1–18; 14:9–12).

The final anti-God order is beastly because it is inhuman in its rebellion against Jehovah. In Daniel, the kingdoms of the world are portrayed as beasts rising from the sea, each marked by predatory power, arrogance, and hostility toward the holy ones (Dan. 7:2–8, 17–25). Revelation takes up that same prophetic pattern and brings it to its climactic form. The beastly order in Revelation is not a random symbol detached from Daniel. It is the mature, final expression of world power energized by Satan, directed against God, and demanding the allegiance that belongs only to Jehovah and to His Christ.

The final conflict is therefore fundamentally theological. Politics, economics, public power, persecution, and propaganda are all involved, but they are not the deepest issue. The beastly order exists to secure worship. The beast does not merely seek compliance. It seeks reverence, submission, identification, and public loyalty. Revelation therefore must be read as a disclosure of the final worship-war between the dragon's order and the kingdom of God.

The Dragon as the Source of Beastly Power

Before the beasts are unveiled, Revelation identifies the deeper source behind them. Revelation 12 describes the great dragon, explicitly identified as "the original serpent, the one called Devil and Satan, who is misleading the whole inhabited earth" (Rev. 12:9). This identification is essential. The final anti-God order is not autonomous. Human rebellion does not mature in isolation. Behind the beastly structure stands the dragon, the ancient enemy of God, the deceiver of the nations, and the adversary of the holy ones.

This means that the final conflict cannot be reduced to mere sociology or political theory. The struggle is not only between one government and another, one ideology and another, or one civilization and another. It is spiritual in source and theological in aim. Satan wages war against the woman, against her seed, and against those "who keep the commandments of God and hold to the testimony of Jesus" (Rev. 12:17). The beastly order is therefore satanic not because it is exotic or mysterious, but because it is anti-God in worship, truth, and allegiance.

The dragon's frustration in Revelation 12 leads directly into Revelation 13. Unable to overthrow the purpose of God, he turns to earthly instruments. He stands on the sand of the sea, and from that turbulent sea the beast arises (Rev. 12:17–13:1). The sea, already familiar from Daniel 7, symbolizes the restless and troubled sphere of the nations out of which beastly world power emerges (Dan. 7:2–3). The final order therefore arises from the world of fallen humanity under satanic energizing, not from the kingdom of God.

The Beast From the Sea

Revelation 13:1–10 introduces the beast from the sea: "And I saw a beast coming up out of the sea, having ten horns and seven heads, and on his horns ten diadems, and on his heads blasphemous names" (Rev. 13:1). The imagery is composite and intentionally linked to Daniel. In Daniel 7, four successive beasts emerge from the sea, representing four kingdoms or empires (Dan. 7:3–7, 17). Revelation gathers those beastly features into one climactic figure. John says the beast was "like a leopard, and his feet were like

Edward D. Andrews

those of a bear, and his mouth like the mouth of a lion" (Rev. 13:2), clearly drawing on the imagery of Daniel's leopard, bear, and lion (Dan. 7:4–6). The final beast is therefore not a new concept detached from prior revelation. It is the mature consolidation of beastly empire in its final anti-God form.

The dragon gives this beast "his power and his throne and great authority" (Rev. 13:2). That statement settles the matter of origin. The beast from the sea is a satanically empowered world order. It does not possess legitimate sovereignty in the ultimate sense. Its authority is derivative, granted within the mysterious limits of divine permission, yet energized by the dragon for rebellion against God.

The beast's seven heads and ten horns signify fullness of authority, ruling structures, and kingly power in concentrated form. Revelation later interprets related imagery in terms of kings and kingdom arrangements (Rev. 17:9–13). The point in chapter 13 is not to invite arithmetic speculation but to portray a complete and formidable anti-God rulership structure. The beast is not a passing local government. It is the final beastly order of world dominion standing against God and His people.

One of the beast's heads appears to have a mortal wound that was healed, and the world marvels and follows the beast (Rev. 13:3). The imagery presents the beast as a counterfeit of resurrection and triumph. It mimics life after death. It appears invincible, recovered, triumphant, and worthy of admiration. This imitation is important. Satan does not merely oppose God by open denial. He counterfeits. The beast presents itself as the answer to the world's instability, as the power that survived its wound and therefore deserves submission. But its apparent triumph is a blasphemous parody, not a true resurrection.

The response of the world is revealing: "they worshiped the dragon because he gave his authority to the beast; and they worshiped the beast, saying, 'Who is like the beast, and who is able to wage war with him?'" (Rev. 13:4). Here the heart of the matter is exposed. The issue is worship. The beast evokes awe, fear, and devotion. Men do not merely obey it as a state apparatus. They revere it as ultimate. In worshiping the beast they worship the dragon behind it. The final anti-God order therefore becomes the visible mediator of satanic allegiance in the world.

The beast is then given "a mouth speaking great things and blasphemies" and authority to act for forty-two months (Rev. 13:5). This again parallels Daniel's arrogant horn that speaks great things against the Most High and persecutes the holy ones for a measured time (Dan. 7:8, 20, 25). The beast opens its mouth "in blasphemies against God, to blaspheme His name and His tabernacle, that is, those who dwell in heaven" (Rev. 13:6). This is not merely harsh rhetoric. It is open, public defiance of God. The beastly order exists in direct opposition to Jehovah's rule and to all who belong to Him.

Revelation adds that the beast was permitted "to make war with the holy ones and to conquer them" and authority was given "over every tribe and people and tongue and nation" (Rev. 13:7). The universality of its reach again shows that this is no narrow local power. It is the final anti-God world structure. Yet even here the text retains divine sovereignty. Authority "was given" to the beast. It is allowed to act for an appointed period, but it is not ultimate. Its triumph is temporary, measured, and doomed.

Those who dwell on the earth worship the beast, "everyone whose name has not been written from the foundation of the world in the book of life of the Lamb who has been slaughtered" (Rev. 13:8). The world is thus divided

Edward D. Andrews

between beast-worshipers and the Lamb's people. Neutrality disappears. Final history is not about private spirituality without public consequence. It is about manifest allegiance.

The Beast From the Earth, the False Prophet

Revelation 13:11–18 introduces the second beast: "Then I saw another beast coming up out of the earth; and he had two horns like a lamb and he was speaking as a dragon" (Rev. 13:11). Later Revelation identifies this second beast as the false prophet (Rev. 16:13; 19:20; 20:10). That title clarifies his religious role. He is not merely a political assistant. He is the propagandist, miracle-worker, and ideological enforcer of beast-worship.

The second beast is especially deceptive because he has "two horns like a lamb." He presents himself with lamb-like appearance. The imagery suggests religious resemblance, counterfeit gentleness, and a false claim to legitimacy. Yet he "speaks as a dragon." His true voice is satanic. This is the essence of false religion in the final conflict. It imitates what is holy while serving what is demonic. It borrows the appearance of truth in order to direct men into worship of the beast.

Revelation says that he "exercises all the authority of the first beast in his presence" and causes the earth and those dwelling in it to worship the first beast (Rev. 13:12). His work is not independent. He is subordinate, but essential. The final anti-God order is not merely coercive government. It is political-religious. The second beast sacralizes the first beast. He teaches the world how to worship power. He interprets beastly authority as worthy of devotion and presents allegiance to the beast as the proper path for mankind.

He also performs "great signs, so that he even makes fire come down out of heaven to the earth before men" (Rev. 13:13). This again shows that the final conflict includes counterfeit wonders. Miraculous display does not prove divine truth. False religion may use signs to deceive, and those signs may be powerful enough to astonish the world. Jesus had already warned that false christs and false prophets would show signs and wonders to mislead, if possible, even the chosen ones (Matt. 24:24). Paul had said the lawless one would come with power, signs, and lying wonders according to Satan's working (2 Thess. 2:9). Revelation agrees. The second beast deceives precisely through spectacle and counterfeit divine-like acts.

The purpose of the signs is explicitly theological: "he deceives those who dwell on the earth because of the signs" and tells them "to make an image to the beast" (Rev. 13:14). The signs do not lead men to repentance, truth, or the fear of Jehovah. They lead them to idolatry. That is the mark of false religion. It does not merely coexist beside worldly power; it sanctifies and enforces it.

The Image of the Beast

The image of the beast is one of the clearest indications that the final conflict is about worship. Revelation says the second beast was granted power "to give breath to the image of the beast, so that the image of the beast would even speak and cause as many as do not worship the image of the beast to be killed" (Rev. 13:15). This language recalls Daniel 3, where Nebuchadnezzar erected a golden image and demanded universal worship under threat of death. Revelation intensifies that pattern into the final anti-God order. Once again, beastly power cannot rest content with political obedience. It requires religious submission.

The image should not be reduced to a mere statue in wooden literalism, nor should it be dissolved into vagueness. The point is institutionalized idolatry. The image represents the beastly order in a form that can receive, mediate, and enforce worship. It is the visible embodiment of the beast's claim upon human allegiance. Whether one emphasizes cultic representation, regime symbolism, or organized structures of enforced devotion, the theological meaning is plain: the beast demands worship and death for those who refuse it.

This makes clear that the final anti-God order is not secular in the modern sense of merely nonreligious public administration. It is pseudo-religious. It claims what belongs to God. It punishes nonconformity not merely as civic disobedience but as refusal of the sacred order it has established. The image therefore belongs to the same logic as the temple-claim of the man of lawlessness in 2 Thessalonians 2:4. The anti-God order exalts itself in the sphere of worship.

This also explains why the faithful suffer. They are not persecuted simply for dissenting from a policy. They are persecuted because they refuse idolatry. Like Daniel's companions before Nebuchadnezzar's image, the holy ones refuse to bow before a power that has crossed the line from government into blasphemous worship-claim (Dan. 3:16–18). The final conflict is therefore covenantal. It is about whether one will worship Jehovah and the Lamb or submit to the beastly counterfeit.

The Mark of the Beast

Revelation continues: "And he causes all, the small and the great, and the rich and the poor, and the free and the slaves, to be given a mark on their right hand or on their forehead" (Rev. 13:16). The mark is then tied to buying and selling: no one can transact unless he has the mark, "the name of the beast or the number of his name" (Rev. 13:17). This is one of the most sensationalized symbols in all of biblical prophecy, yet the text itself provides the theological framework necessary to avoid distortion.

The first and most important point is that the mark belongs to the worship context of Revelation 13–14. It is not introduced as a neutral device or as a merely economic mechanism. It is inseparable from beast-worship. Those who worship the beast and his image receive the mark (Rev. 14:9–11; 16:2; 19:20; 20:4). The mark therefore signifies belonging, allegiance, and identification. It is the beast's claim upon the person in thought and deed.

The placement on the forehead and hand is not accidental. In biblical thought, the forehead is associated with identity, confession, and visible belonging, while the hand is associated with action and obedience. The law of God was to be bound as a sign on the hand and as frontlets between the eyes, signifying total covenant loyalty in thought and conduct (Exod. 13:9, 16; Deut. 6:6–8; 11:18). Revelation itself contrasts the servants of God, who bear His name on their foreheads, with the worshipers of the beast, who bear his mark (Rev. 7:3; 14:1; 22:4). The mark of the beast is therefore the satanic counter-sign to the divine seal. It is a symbol of covenantal belonging to the anti-God order.

This means the mark is not first about technology. It is first about worship and allegiance. Economic coercion is real, but it is secondary in theological order. The beastly system uses commerce as an enforcement mechanism. It pressures the conscience by linking participation in public economic life to submission to beastly authority. Yet Revelation's concern is deeper than commercial restriction. The issue is whether men will give their thought and action to the beast or remain loyal to God.

This theological priority must govern interpretation. Whenever the mark is reduced to speculation about microchips, currencies, medical procedures, or ordinary tools without reference to worship and idolatry, the symbol is stripped from its biblical setting. Revelation does not present the mark as a random technological fear. It presents it as the visible sign of beastly allegiance imposed within a final anti-God political-religious order.

The Number of the Beast: 666

Revelation closes the section by saying, "Here is wisdom. Let the one who has understanding calculate the number of the beast, for it is the number of a man, and his number is six hundred and sixty-six" (Rev. 13:18). The verse calls for wisdom, not panic. The number is associated with the beast and with man. The point is not to encourage endless code-cracking detached from the theology of the passage. The number reveals the character of the beastly order as man in consummate rebellion.

Six, falling short of seven, signifies incompleteness and human deficiency when viewed against divine fullness. Repeated in triple form, 666 intensifies that meaning. It is the mature number of man, not God; of the creature exalting itself, not the Creator; of false greatness collapsing under judgment. The beastly order presents itself as ultimate, but its number exposes it as fundamentally human, creaturely, and doomed. It is man organized against God in the fullness of his rebellion, yet still falling short of divine perfection.

The text says it is "the number of a man," which reinforces this theological reading. The beast may appear overwhelming, global, and quasi-divine, but Revelation interprets it as man in blasphemous self-exaltation. It is the final anti-God order of humanity energized by Satan, claiming sacred status, but still numbered as man. Its pretended immortality, invincibility, and majesty are therefore lies. Its number exposes its limitation and its judgment.

The Beastly Order as Political-Religious Totality

When Revelation 13 is read as a whole, the picture is coherent. The dragon is the source. The beast from the sea is the final anti-God dominion in its political-religious majesty. The beast from the earth, the false prophet, is the religious propagandist and deceiver who directs the world to worship the first beast. The image of the beast is the visible and institutionalized embodiment of that worship-demand. The mark of the beast is the sign of allegiance, imposed in thought and action and reinforced through economic coercion. The number 666 interprets the whole structure as man in consummate rebellion.

This means the beastly order should not be interpreted as merely political. It is political-religious totality. Government, ideology, public worship, false signs, propaganda, and economic pressure are all fused together into one final anti-God system. It is this totality that makes the conflict final. The beast does not merely command armies. It commands conscience. It does not merely levy taxes. It claims worship. It does not merely enforce law. It defines reality, punishes dissent, and sanctifies its own authority.

This is why Revelation 13 must be read beside 2 Thessalonians 2. The man of lawlessness exalts himself in the sphere of worship and is destroyed by the appearing of Christ (2 Thess. 2:3–8). The beastly order claims worship, persecutes the holy ones, and is overthrown by the rider on the white horse (Rev. 13:7–8; 19:11–21). The categories are distinct, but they converge on the same final anti-God rebellion. The apostasy, the lawless one, the beastly order, and the false prophet belong to the same broad conflict, though Scripture preserves each figure's own theological function.

The Faithful in the Final Conflict

Revelation does not describe the beastly order merely to identify evil. It describes it so that the faithful will know how to endure. In the midst of the chapter's terrifying imagery, John says, "Here is the endurance and the faith of the holy ones" (Rev. 13:10). Later he says, "Here is the endurance of the holy ones, those who keep the commandments of God and the faith of Jesus" (Rev. 14:12). Endurance is possible because the beast's power is temporary, measured, and judged. The holy ones are not called to conquer by sword, but by faithfulness.

Revelation even says that some refuse the mark and do not worship the beast or his image, though it costs them dearly (Rev. 20:4). The final conflict therefore reveals the true nature of discipleship. It is not merely inward conviction. It is public loyalty to God in the face of public pressure. Worship cannot be divided. Either men worship God and the Lamb or they yield to the beastly order.

This is why the chapter must never be handled as religious sensationalism. Revelation 13 is not meant to produce obsession with speculative details while neglecting the central demand of the passage. It is meant to strengthen believers to remain loyal when the anti-God order claims what belongs only to Jehovah. The chapter is a call to discernment, courage, and steadfastness.

The Beast and the Certainty of Christ's Triumph

However formidable the beastly order appears, Revelation never allows it the final word. The beast makes war with the holy ones, deceives the nations, and compels worship, but his authority is temporary. He is energized by the dragon, but the dragon is already a defeated enemy on borrowed time. Revelation 17–19 makes the outcome plain: the beast turns even against Babylon under God's overruling purpose (Rev. 17:16–17), gathers the kings of the earth for final rebellion, and is then seized and cast into the lake of fire with the false prophet at the coming of Christ (Rev. 19:19–20).

The final conflict is therefore not uncertain. The beastly order rises only to be judged. The false prophet performs signs only to be exposed. The image enforces worship only until the true King appears. The mark distinguishes the beast's worshipers only until divine judgment falls upon them. The number 666 declares the beastly order's human pretension only until Christ reveals its frailty by destroying it.

The church must therefore read Revelation 13 with sobriety, but also with confidence. The final anti-God order is real. It is political, religious, coercive, and global in aspiration. It demands worship and punishes refusal. Yet it is not ultimate. It is beastly, not divine. It is numbered as man, not God. It is empowered by the dragon, but destroyed by the Lamb. Its conflict with the holy ones is fierce, but temporary. Christ's victory is decisive, and the beastly order will not survive the appearing of the King.

Chapter 7 — The Visible Return of Jesus Christ

The Return of Christ as Public Manifestation

The Second Coming of Jesus Christ is not a hidden event, an inward spiritual experience, or a symbolic way of describing the gradual triumph of Christian influence in history. Scripture presents it as the public manifestation of the risen and reigning Lord. The same Jesus who was seen, heard, crucified, raised, and taken up into heaven will return openly in divine authority and glory. The New Testament does not allow His return to be reduced to metaphor. It is a literal, visible, historical event that brings the present rebellious order to its appointed end.

Jesus Himself said, "then the sign of the Son of Man will appear in heaven, and then all the tribes of the earth will mourn, and they will see the Son of Man coming on the clouds of heaven with power and great glory" (Matt. 24:30). That statement is decisive. His return is not secret. "They will see" Him. It is not local or private. "All the tribes of the earth will mourn." It is not weak or symbolic. He comes "with power and great glory." The words of Christ leave no room for a doctrine that turns His coming into a hidden heavenly shift or an invisible phase known only to a few.

The same truth is confirmed at the ascension. As the disciples looked intently into heaven while Jesus was taken up, two angels declared, "This Jesus who has been taken up from you into heaven will come in just the same way as you have watched Him go into heaven" (Acts 1:11). The force of the promise lies in its plainness. He ascended personally, visibly, and bodily. He will return personally, visibly, and bodily. The disciples did not merely sense His departure inwardly. They watched Him go. The promise therefore demands a corresponding return. The ascension and the Second Coming are bound together in the same historical realism.

The apostle Paul speaks in the same way. "For the Lord Himself will descend from heaven with a shout, with the voice of an archangel and with the trumpet of God" (1 Thess. 4:16). The phrase "the Lord Himself" excludes every attempt to reduce the event to delegated agency or vague spiritual influence. The shout, the voice of an archangel, and the trumpet of God exclude secrecy. This is not a quiet event hidden from the world. It is divine intervention. It is heaven breaking into history in public authority. The church is not waiting for a private sign in the heart, but for the visible descent of the Lord from heaven.

Revelation 19 provides the same portrait in apocalyptic form. John says, "I saw heaven opened, and look, a white horse, and the one seated on it is called Faithful and True, and in righteousness He judges and wages war" (Rev. 19:11). Heaven opens. The barrier between heavenly decree and earthly execution is removed in the vision. The Messiah appears as the righteous warrior-king. He is not hidden. He is not implied. He comes forth openly against the beastly order. This is the public appearing of Christ in judgment.

The Glory of the Coming King

The visible return of Christ is also a glorious return. The One who came the first time in humility, who was despised and rejected, will come again in royal majesty. The first coming revealed the suffering Messiah. The second reveals the reigning Messiah. Both belong to the same Christ, but they do not manifest the same phase of His mission. At His first coming He took the form of a servant and humbled Himself even to death on a cross (Phil. 2:6–8). At His second coming He appears in the glory that belongs to the exalted Son of Man and King of kings.

Jesus says He comes "with power and great glory" (Matt. 24:30). Mark says the same: "then they will see the Son of Man coming in clouds with great power and glory" (Mark 13:26). Luke adds that believers are to lift up their heads because their redemption draws near when these things begin to occur (Luke 21:27–28). The cloud imagery is not decorative. It belongs to the language of divine manifestation and kingdom authority. Daniel had already seen "One like a Son of Man" coming "with the clouds of heaven" and receiving dominion, glory, and a kingdom that all peoples should serve Him (Dan. 7:13–14). Jesus takes that language to Himself. His return is therefore the public manifestation of the heavenly authority already granted to Him.

Revelation 19 expands the same glory. His eyes are a flame of fire. On His head are many diadems. He is clothed in an outer garment sprinkled with blood. His name is called The Word of God. He comes with the armies of heaven, and on His garment and on His thigh a name is written: "King of kings and Lord of lords" (Rev. 19:12–16). Every feature of the passage magnifies His royal supremacy. The many diadems signify comprehensive kingship, in contrast to the limited and usurping crowns of the dragon and the beast. The flaming eyes signify penetrating judgment. The name "Faithful and True" interprets His appearing: He comes in perfect consistency with all that God has promised and warned.

This glory also shows why the world mourns. The coming of Christ is not merely inspiring. It is terrifying to the rebellious. Men may speak confidently against God now. Rulers may boast. The beastly order may demand allegiance. But when the true King appears, all false sovereignty is exposed as empty. The tribes of the earth mourn because the age of rebellion ends when He is manifested.

The Return Is Unmistakable

Jesus repeatedly taught that His return will be unmistakable. This was necessary because deception is one of the central features of the last days. False christs, false prophets, and false claims about the nearness or hidden presence of the end would arise (Matt. 24:4–5, 11, 23–26). The Lord therefore defined the true nature of His coming in terms that destroy all counterfeit expectations. "For just as the lightning comes from the east and shines as far as the west, so will the presence of the Son of Man be" (Matt. 24:27).

Lightning is not secret. It is sudden, public, and impossible to confine to some hidden chamber. Jesus even says, "if they say to you, 'Look, He is in the wilderness,' do not go out, or, 'Look, He is in the inner rooms,' do not believe them" (Matt. 24:26). That warning is decisive against every doctrine that locates Christ's return in a hidden place, a private revelation, or a concealed heavenly event detached from visible manifestation. The real return of Christ does not need to be discovered through rumor. It will be seen.

Paul agrees. The Lord descends with public signs of command and authority (1 Thess. 4:16). Peter agrees. The day of the Lord comes like a thief in the sense of suddenness for the unprepared, but it is accompanied by cosmic judgment and the passing away of the present order (2 Pet. 3:10). John agrees. "Every eye will see Him" (Rev. 1:7). The apostolic doctrine therefore rests on one unified certainty: the coming of Christ is open, undeniable, and universal in significance.

This also means there is no room for a two-stage return in which Christ first comes secretly for believers and only later appears openly to the world. The New Testament consistently speaks of one appearing, one revelation, one descent, one παρουσία of Christ in which He comes in glory, gathers His people, judges His enemies, and advances His kingdom. The same event that is comfort for believers is terror for the rebellious. The same appearing that raises the dead in Christ brings destruction upon the anti-God order. Scripture never divides these realities into disconnected comings.

Edward D. Andrews

The Gathering of Believers at His Appearing

The visible return of Christ is not only an event of judgment. It is also the great gathering of His people. Jesus says that after the cosmic upheaval and the appearing of the Son of Man, "He will send forth His angels with a great trumpet and they will gather together His chosen ones from the four winds, from one end of the sky to the other" (Matt. 24:31). This gathering is directly connected to His visible coming. It is not a hidden event occurring years earlier. The Son of Man appears, the trumpet sounds, and the chosen ones are gathered.

Paul gives the same sequence in 1 Thessalonians 4. The Lord descends from heaven, the dead in Christ rise first, and then "we who are alive, who remain, will be caught up together with them in the clouds to meet the Lord in the air; and so we will always be with the Lord" (1 Thess. 4:17). The gathering includes both the resurrected dead and the transformed living. It is one united event. The dead are not left behind. The living do not receive some separate salvation detached from them. Christ's appearing gathers all who belong to Him.

This is why Paul begins that section by addressing grief. Believers were mourning those who had died, and Paul comforts them not with the doctrine of an immortal soul already enjoying fullness of life, but with the certainty of resurrection at Christ's return (1 Thess. 4:13–16). The hope of the church is resurrection and gathering at the appearing of the Lord. The dead in Christ rise first. Then the living are transformed and assembled together with them.

The same doctrine appears in 1 Corinthians 15. Paul says, "each in his own order: Christ the firstfruits, afterward those who are Christ's at His coming" (1 Cor. 15:23). He then explains, "we will not all sleep, but we will all be changed, in a moment, in the twinkling of an eye, at the last trumpet" (1 Cor. 15:51–52). The dead are raised imperishable, and the living are transformed. Again the return is public, trumpet-accompanied, resurrection-centered, and final in its effect upon the faithful. Yet the future life granted at that time is not described in one identical way for all the righteous. The heavenly co-rulers receive immortality, while the broader righteous receive everlasting life under God's kingdom.

The language of meeting the Lord in the air should not be twisted into a doctrine of permanent removal from all kingdom realities connected with the earth. The emphasis is on union with Christ at His royal arrival. The faithful go out to meet the returning Lord and belong to Him forever. The passage does not teach an escape from the kingdom. It teaches participation in the triumph of the King.

The Return and the Resurrection of the Dead

The visible return of Christ cannot be separated from the resurrection. Jesus Himself tied the final hope to resurrection "on the last day" (John 6:39–40, 44, 54). He said, "an hour is coming, in which all who are in the tombs will hear His voice, and will come out" (John 5:28–29). The language is clear. Those in the tombs are not described as presently living in conscious blessedness apart from resurrection. They are in the tombs, awaiting the voice of the Son.

Paul's teaching in 1 Corinthians 15 confirms the same truth. If the dead are not raised, then Christ Himself has not been raised, preaching is vain, and faith is empty (1 Cor. 15:12–19). But Christ has been raised as the firstfruits, and therefore those who belong to Him will be raised at His coming (1 Cor. 15:20–23). The resurrection does not occur independently of the return. It is part of the return. It is one of the chief reasons the church waits for Christ.

This point matters because the Second Coming is often detached from the doctrine of death and resurrection in popular teaching. Yet the apostolic pattern refuses that separation. The believer's hope is not simply to depart this world and enter immediate fullness elsewhere. The believer's hope is the appearing of Jesus Christ, the raising of the dead, the transformation of the living, and the defeat of death itself. But even here Scripture preserves a distinction: not all who are raised to life receive immortality. Immortality belongs to those raised for heavenly reign with Christ, whereas everlasting life is granted to the righteous who live under His kingdom rule. The return of Christ is therefore not only a royal event but a life-giving event. It is the hour when the voice of the Son summons the dead who belong to Him.

The Return as the End of the Lawless Rebellion

The appearing of Christ also brings the rebellion of the lawless and beastly powers to an end. Paul states this with unmistakable force: "then that lawless one will be revealed, whom the Lord Jesus will slay with the breath of His mouth and bring to nothing by the appearance of His coming" (2 Thess. 2:8). The lawless one is not gradually weakened by historical change or defeated by human reform. He is brought to nothing by the visible appearing of Jesus Christ.

The phrase "the appearance of His coming" emphasizes the open manifestation of the event. The lawless one's destruction is tied directly to Christ's epiphany. This means the final apostasy and self-exalting anti-God rebellion meet their decisive end at the return of Christ. There is no room here for the notion that Christ returns secretly while lawlessness continues openly for some extended period. Paul's sequence is straightforward: apostasy, unveiling of lawlessness, appearing of Christ, destruction of lawlessness.

The imagery of "the breath of His mouth" echoes Isaiah 11:4, where the Messianic ruler slays the wicked with the breath of His lips. Christ judges by sovereign word. He does not struggle against the lawless one as though the outcome were in doubt. His appearing itself is enough to end the pretended majesty of the usurper.

Revelation 19 presents the same reality in apocalyptic imagery. The beast, the kings of the earth, and their armies are gathered to make war against the rider on the white horse and His army (Rev. 19:19). Yet the conflict is not prolonged. "The beast was taken, and with him the false prophet that performed the signs in his sight" (Rev. 19:20). The false prophet had deceived those who received the mark of the beast and worshiped his image. Political rebellion and false religion therefore fall together under Christ's judgment. The beast and the false prophet are cast alive into the lake of fire, and the rest are slain by the sword proceeding from the mouth of the rider (Rev. 19:20–21).

This is the final answer to the beastly order. The anti-God system may appear immense, global, and invincible within history, but its downfall is immediate before the appearing of the King. The nations gather. The beast boasts. The false prophet deceives. The mark divides humanity by allegiance. Yet when Christ comes, all of it collapses. The lawless rebellion does not survive His appearing.

The Return as the Defeat of the Beastly Order

The beast from the sea, the false prophet, the image of the beast, and the mark of the beast all belong to the final anti-God order described in Revelation 13. That order is fundamentally about worship and allegiance, not mere politics. The beast demands what belongs only to God. The false prophet directs the world into worship of the beast. The image institutionalizes idolatry. The mark signifies belonging to that order in thought and action. Revelation 19 shows the end of that entire system.

The rider on the white horse comes "in righteousness" to judge and wage war (Rev. 19:11). He is called Faithful and True. His many diadems show comprehensive kingship. His robe dipped in blood signifies judicial majesty and victorious advance. From His mouth comes a sharp sword with which to strike the nations, and "He will shepherd them with a rod of iron" (Rev. 19:15). This fulfills Psalm 2:9, where Jehovah promises His Anointed that He will break the rebellious nations with an iron scepter.

The kings of the earth and their armies gather together, but the beast is seized, the false prophet is seized with him, and the rebellion is crushed (Rev. 19:19–21). Revelation has spent much time unveiling the arrogance and deception of the beastly coalition, but when Christ appears, its destruction is immediate. This brevity is theological. The final conflict may look formidable from the earth, but before the Lord of glory it is no contest. The outcome was never in doubt. The beastly order is exposed as temporary, derivative, and doomed.

Thus the visible return of Christ is the end of the final anti-God political-religious system. The man of lawlessness is destroyed. The beast and false prophet are judged. The rebellious kings are overthrown. The anti-God order that claimed worship is shattered by the true King whose appearing no rival can survive.

The Return and the Beginning of the Kingdom's Next Stage

The destruction of the lawless and beastly powers at Christ's return is not the end of all kingdom action. It is the transition into the next stage of Christ's reign. Revelation 19 flows into Revelation 20. The beast and false prophet are judged, then Satan is bound, and then those who share in the first resurrection reign with Christ for a thousand years (Rev. 20:1–6). The sequence matters. Christ returns before the thousand-year reign, not after it. The visible return is therefore both the end of the present rebellious order and the beginning of the millennial kingdom administration.

Paul's teaching also fits this structure. Christ comes, those who are His are raised at His coming, then comes the ordered defeat of all enemies until death itself is abolished (1 Cor. 15:23–26). The appearing of Christ is not an isolated flash of glory without kingdom consequence. It is the decisive intervention by which all the promises of divine rule move toward fulfillment.

This also means the return of Christ cannot be reduced to a symbolic way of speaking about His present heavenly reign. He reigns now at the right hand of God, but Scripture also teaches a future appearing in which He judges openly, raises the dead, destroys His enemies, and advances His kingdom in manifested power. The present heavenly reign and the future visible return are not contradictory. They are successive phases in the one kingship of Christ.

The Church's Confidence in the Coming King

The doctrine of the visible return of Jesus Christ is therefore one of comfort, warning, and certainty. It comforts because believers know their Lord Himself will descend from heaven, the dead in Christ will rise, and the faithful will be gathered to Him. It warns because the rebellious world, the lawless one, and the beastly order will face the public judgment of the returning King. It gives certainty because no anti-God power, however impressive now, will survive the appearance of Christ.

This is why the New Testament calls believers to watchfulness rather than fear. The coming of Christ will be sudden for the unprepared, but it will not be hidden. It will be public and unmistakable. The faithful do not need secret reports, private revelations, or speculative systems to know their Lord has returned. They wait for the One whom every eye will see. They wait for the Son of Man who comes on the clouds with power and great glory. They wait for the Lord who descends with a shout, the voice of an archangel, and the trumpet of God. They wait for the rider on the white horse whose appearing ends the rebellion of the lawless and beastly powers forever.

The visible return of Jesus Christ is therefore the great historical manifestation of His kingship. It is the moment when heaven opens, the King appears, the dead are raised, the faithful are gathered, the wicked are judged, the beastly order is broken, and the kingdom advances under the sovereign decree of Jehovah. In that coming order, the select resurrected holy ones receive immortality for heavenly rule, while the broader righteous receive everlasting life according to God's purpose for the earth. It is not a secondary doctrine. It is the great appearing toward which the apostolic church looked and for which the faithful still wait.

Edward D. Andrews

Chapter 8 — The Resurrection of the Dead

Resurrection as the Heart of Christian Hope

The biblical doctrine of resurrection stands at the center of the Christian hope. It is not a secondary feature of the faith, nor a poetic way of speaking about survival after death. It is the divinely revealed answer to death itself. Scripture does not teach that man possesses an immortal soul that continues in conscious existence independent of the body. It teaches that man dies, returns to the dust, and awaits resurrection by the power of God (Gen. 2:7; 3:19; Eccl. 9:5, 10; Dan. 12:2; John 5:28–29). Life beyond death is therefore not natural possession. It is divine gift. Eternal life is granted through God's resurrecting power in Christ.

This truth is foundational to the gospel. If death is only the shedding of a bodily shell while the real person remains fully alive elsewhere, then resurrection is no longer central. It becomes an unnecessary appendage. But Scripture will not allow that. The New Testament insists that if the dead are not raised, then Christ Himself has not been raised, preaching is vain, faith is futile, and believers are still in their sins (1 Cor. 15:13–17). Resurrection is therefore not an optional doctrine. It is the necessary outworking of redemption and the necessary defeat of death.

The Christian hope is not that death is harmless. Death is an enemy (1 Cor. 15:26). It is the wages of sin (Rom. 6:23). It is the return of the human person to dust and silence apart from divine intervention (Ps. 146:4; Eccl. 12:7). But the gospel announces that Jehovah has acted in Christ to conquer this enemy. Jesus died, was buried, and was raised on the third day according to the Scriptures (1 Cor. 15:3–4). His resurrection is not merely proof of His divine mission. It is the firstfruits and guarantee of the future resurrection of those who belong to Him (1 Cor. 15:20, 23).

For that reason, the doctrine of the resurrection of the dead is inseparable from the doctrine of the return of Christ. The dead are raised at His coming. The righteous are not made complete by death itself, but by the appearing of the Lord who calls them from the grave (John 6:39–40, 44, 54; 1 Cor. 15:23; 1 Thess. 4:16). The final hope of believers is therefore not departure into an immaterial state, but resurrection into the life God appoints under His kingdom.

Man Is a Soul, Not the Possessor of an Immortal Soul

A right doctrine of resurrection depends on a right doctrine of man. Scripture does not say that man has a soul in the Greek philosophical sense of an immortal, conscious essence trapped temporarily in the body. It says that man became a soul. Genesis 2:7 states, "Jehovah God formed man from dust of the ground, and breathed into his nostrils the breath of life; and the man became a living soul." Man is a unified creature formed from dust and animated by the breath of life. The soul in biblical language is the living person, not an indestructible inner substance that can never die.

This is confirmed throughout Scripture. Ezekiel says plainly, "the soul who sins shall die" (Ezek. 18:4, 20). Joshua speaks of souls being destroyed in judgment (Josh. 10:28–39). The Psalms use soul language for mortal life vulnerable to death, danger, and destruction (Ps. 22:20; 33:19; 78:50). Jesus Himself says that God can destroy both soul and body in Gehenna (Matt. 10:28). None of this fits the claim that the soul is by nature immortal and indestructible.

The book of Ecclesiastes reinforces the same doctrine. "The living know that they will die; but the dead know nothing at all" (Eccl. 9:5). Again, "there is no work or plan or knowledge or wisdom in Sheol, where you are going" (Eccl. 9:10). These are not the words of a worldview in which the dead remain fully conscious in another realm. They describe death as cessation of active human life and consciousness. The grave is not a place of ongoing earthly thought and action. It is the condition from which only God can restore the dead.

The New Testament follows the same pattern. Jesus described Lazarus as sleeping in death before raising him (John 11:11–14). Paul repeatedly refers to the Christian dead as those who have "fallen asleep" (1 Cor. 15:6, 18, 20, 51; 1 Thess. 4:13–15). The metaphor of sleep does not suggest conscious activity in another sphere. It emphasizes the temporary state of death in view of coming awakening by divine power.

For this reason, the doctrine of resurrection is not an embellishment added to a doctrine of natural immortality. It is the biblical alternative to it. Man does not possess indestructible life by nature. Eternal life is God's gift in Christ (Rom. 6:23). Resurrection is therefore essential because death is real. If the dead are to live again, God must raise them.

The Old Testament Foundation of Resurrection Hope

The resurrection of the dead is not first introduced in the New Testament. It rests upon Old Testament revelation, though that revelation comes into clearer focus over time. The faith of the Old Testament is not centered on the immortality of the soul, but on Jehovah's power over death and His faithfulness to restore life.

Job expresses this hope in profound terms: "after my skin has been destroyed, yet from my flesh I shall see God" (Job 19:26). Whatever interpretive debates surround the precise wording, the text clearly points beyond death toward a future vindication in relation to God. Abraham's willingness to offer Isaac was grounded in confidence that God could raise the dead (Heb. 11:17–19), showing that resurrection hope was already implicit in patriarchal faith.

The Psalms also contain seeds of resurrection hope. Psalm 16:10 says, "you will not abandon my soul to Sheol, nor will you allow your Holy One to see corruption." In its fullest sense this is fulfilled in Christ's resurrection (Acts 2:25–31; 13:35–37), but it also reveals that the grave is not beyond Jehovah's power. Psalm 49 contrasts the death of the wicked with the hope of the righteous, declaring, "God will redeem my soul from the power of Sheol, for He will receive me" (Ps. 49:15). Psalm 73 looks beyond present injustice to final divine nearness and vindication (Ps. 73:23–26).

The clearest Old Testament statement appears in Daniel 12:2: "many of those sleeping in the dust of the ground will awake, these to everlasting life, but the others to reproach and everlasting contempt." Here the language is explicit. The dead are sleeping in the dust. They are not active as conscious spirits elsewhere. They awake by divine intervention. The outcome is twofold: life for some, shame and judgment for others. Daniel thus provides the essential structure later developed in the New Testament: death, divine intervention, resurrection, and divergent everlasting outcomes.

Isaiah also points in this direction. "Your dead will live; my corpses will rise. Awake and shout for joy, you who dwell in the dust" (Isa. 26:19). Later Isaiah 25:8 declares that Jehovah "will swallow up death forever." These promises are not philosophical reflections on human indestructibility. They are covenantal promises that Jehovah will act to overthrow death and restore His people.

Thus the Old Testament foundation is clear. The hope of the faithful is not that death is unreal, but that Jehovah will conquer it. The dead rest in the dust until He calls them forth.

Jesus and the Resurrection of the Dead

Jesus' own teaching confirms and intensifies this resurrection doctrine. He did not teach innate human immortality. He taught resurrection at the appointed time. In John 5:28–29 He declares, "an hour is coming, in which all who are in the tombs will hear His voice, and will come out; those who did the good deeds to a resurrection of life, those who committed the evil deeds to a resurrection of judgment." The dead are in the tombs. Their hope lies in His voice. The division of outcome follows resurrection, not independent conscious destiny before it.

John 6 is especially important. Four times Jesus says that He will raise the faithful "on the last day" (John 6:39–40, 44, 54). This repeated phrase leaves no doubt about the timing. The faithful are not portrayed as receiving their final life in full at the moment of death. They are raised on the last day by Christ. This is the language of resurrection hope, not immortal-soul theology.

When Martha says of Lazarus, "I know that he will rise again in the resurrection on the last day," Jesus does not correct her expectation (John 11:24). He confirms it, while centering it in Himself: "I am the resurrection and the life" (John 11:25). Then He raises Lazarus as a sign of His authority over death. Lazarus did not return from endless conscious heavenly life. He was restored from death by the word of Christ.

Jesus also debated the Sadducees on this very issue. Since they denied the resurrection, He answered them from the Scriptures, declaring that Jehovah is "not the God of the dead, but of the living" (Matt. 22:31–32; Mark 12:26–27; Luke 20:37–38). His argument rests on covenant faithfulness and divine power. The patriarchs must live again because Jehovah remains their God. The point is not that they are naturally immortal, but that God's covenant faithfulness requires their restoration.

Thus Jesus places resurrection at the heart of final hope. He does not direct the faithful to trust in a naturally indestructible soul. He directs them to trust in Himself, the One who will call the dead from their graves.

Christ's Resurrection as Firstfruits

The resurrection of Jesus Christ is the decisive event that guarantees the resurrection of the dead. Paul writes, "But now Christ has been raised from the dead, the firstfruits of those who have fallen asleep" (1 Cor. 15:20). The image of firstfruits comes from the first portion of the harvest offered to God, signifying that more of the same harvest must follow. Christ's resurrection is therefore not an isolated miracle detached from His people. It is the beginning of the resurrection harvest.

Paul continues: "For since by a man came death, by a man came also the resurrection of the dead. For as in Adam all die, so also in Christ all will be made alive. But each in his own order: Christ the firstfruits, afterward those who are Christ's at His coming" (1 Cor. 15:21–23). This sequence is crucial. Christ first. Then those who belong to Him at His coming. Resurrection is ordered, Christ-centered, and eschatological.

The phrase "those who are Christ's at His coming" destroys the notion that the dead receive the fullness of resurrection life at death. Their resurrection belongs to the Parousia, the visible return of Christ. This is why Paul comforts the Thessalonians as he does. "The dead in Christ will rise first" when "the Lord Himself will descend from heaven" (1 Thess. 4:16). Resurrection is tied to His return, not detached from it.

Because Christ has been raised, death is no longer the final word. But because resurrection awaits the coming of

Christ, believers still live in hope. The church exists between firstfruits and harvest. The resurrection of Jesus is accomplished fact. The resurrection of His people is certain future.

First Corinthians 15 and the Defeat of Death

No chapter in Scripture develops the doctrine of resurrection more fully than 1 Corinthians 15. Paul writes because some at Corinth were denying the resurrection of the dead (1 Cor. 15:12). He answers by showing that such denial destroys the Christian faith itself. If there is no resurrection of the dead, then Christ has not been raised. If Christ has not been raised, apostolic preaching is empty, faith is vain, the apostles are false witnesses, believers remain in their sins, the dead in Christ have perished, and Christians are of all men most to be pitied (1 Cor. 15:13–19).

This argument shows how central resurrection is. Christianity is not merely a moral system or a religious philosophy. It stands or falls with God's victory over death in Christ and in those who belong to Christ.

Paul then unfolds the victory: "then comes the end, when He hands over the kingdom to the God and Father, when He has abolished all rule and all authority and power. For He must reign until He has put all His enemies under His feet. The last enemy that will be abolished is death" (1 Cor. 15:24–26). Death is not natural friend but enemy. Its abolition is essential to God's final purpose.

The resurrection of the dead is therefore part of a wider kingdom victory. Christ reigns until all enemies are put under His feet. The destruction of death is one of the greatest acts of that reign. Resurrection is not an isolated event. It is the kingdom's assault upon the final enemy.

Paul later asks, "How are the dead raised? And with what kind of body do they come?" (1 Cor. 15:35). His answer is built on transformation, continuity of identity, and divine creative power. What is sown is not what shall be. A seed is sown bare, but God gives it a body as He wills (1 Cor. 15:36–38). Likewise, the body is sown perishable, dishonorable, and weak; it is raised imperishable, glorious, and powerful (1 Cor. 15:42–43). The resurrection body is not a mere resuscitation of the mortal condition. It is a transformed body suited to the life God grants.

Natural Body and Spiritual Body

Paul's distinction between the "natural body" and the "spiritual body" in 1 Corinthians 15:44 has often been misunderstood. He is not contrasting physical body with nonphysical existence. He is contrasting the body as now fitted for mortal earthly life with the body as then fitted for Spirit-governed resurrection life. The resurrection body is still body, but transformed. It is not a vaporous soul-state. It is a divinely given mode of embodied life corresponding to the resurrection order.

Paul grounds this in Adam and Christ. "The first man Adam became a living soul. The last Adam became a life-giving spirit" (1 Cor. 15:45). The first man is from the earth, earthy. The second man is from heaven (1 Cor. 15:47). As believers have borne the image of the earthy one, they will bear the image of the heavenly one (1 Cor. 15:49). Resurrection therefore is participation in the life-order of the risen Christ.

This passage does not teach that believers become disembodied spirits. It teaches that resurrection life is determined by the risen Christ and by the Holy Spirit's power. The "spiritual body" is a body animated, ruled, and fitted by the Spirit for the age to come.

Immortality and Eternal Life Are Not the Same Thing

At this point careful distinction is necessary. Scripture does not use immortality and eternal life as though they were simply interchangeable in every case. Paul says, "this mortal must put on immortality" and "when this mortal has put on immortality, then will come about the saying that is written, 'Death has been swallowed up in victory'" (1 Cor. 15:53–54). The language of immortality here must not be generalized carelessly to every saved person without distinction.

Immortality denotes indestructible life, deathlessness in the full and strict sense. Eternal life denotes unending life, but not necessarily with the same emphasis on inherent indestructibility. Scripture therefore preserves a difference in description. The heavenly co-rulers who share in the first resurrection receive immortality in connection with their heavenly reign with Christ. Revelation 20:4–6 speaks of those who come to life and reign with Christ for a thousand years, declaring, "Blessed and holy is the one who has a part in the first resurrection; over these the second death has no authority." Paul's language in 1 Corinthians 15 fits this reigning company in the most direct way.

By contrast, Scripture also speaks broadly of eternal life as the inheritance of the righteous. "Whoever believes in Him will not be destroyed but have eternal life" (John 3:16). Jesus says the righteous go away "into eternal life" (Matt. 25:46). Daniel 12:2 speaks of resurrection "to everlasting life." Eternal life is therefore the gift granted to the righteous under God's kingdom. It is real, unending life from God, but Scripture does not require that every recipient be described in exactly the same terms as those granted immortality for heavenly rule.

This distinction must be preserved. Not all the saved receive the same future assignment. Some are granted the heavenly calling and reign with Christ. Others receive everlasting life under God's righteous kingdom. Scripture never teaches that all receive immortality in the same sense. Nor does it teach that every future reward is collapsed into one undifferentiated form of existence.

The First Resurrection and the Reigning Company

Revelation 20 provides the key New Testament passage for the first resurrection. John sees those who had remained faithful in the face of beastly persecution. "They came to life and reigned with Christ for a thousand years" (Rev. 20:4). He then says, "This is the first resurrection" (Rev. 20:5). The participants are declared blessed and holy. Over them the second death has no authority. They are priests of God and of Christ and reign with Him for a thousand years (Rev. 20:6).

This passage identifies a select company sharing in heavenly rule with Christ. The language is priestly and royal. It corresponds to the New Testament teaching that there is a heavenly calling and a reigning company associated with Christ's kingdom administration (Luke 12:32; 22:28–30; Rev. 5:9–10; 14:1–4). These are the ones for whom immortality language is most directly appropriate. Their life is secured beyond the power of the second death, and their role is tied to heavenly reign.

This must not be confused with the broader biblical promise of life for the righteous under God's kingdom. The first resurrection is not simply another way of speaking about every future grant of life. It is the resurrection of the blessed and holy who reign with Christ. Scripture marks it out distinctly and connects it directly with kingly and priestly participation in His rule.

The Broader Hope of Everlasting Life

The broader hope held out in Scripture is everlasting life under God's kingdom. This is the language used repeatedly in both Old and New Testaments. Daniel 12:2 speaks of resurrection to everlasting life. John 3:16 promises eternal life to the believer. Matthew 25:46 places the righteous in eternal life over against the wicked going away into punishment. Psalm 37 promises that the righteous will inherit the earth and dwell in it forever (Ps. 37:9, 11, 29). Isaiah envisions renewed conditions of peace, blessing, and longevity under Jehovah's righteous administration (Isa. 11:6–9; 65:17–25). Revelation closes with the New Jerusalem, the river of life, the tree of life, and the healed nations under the light of God and the Lamb (Rev. 21:1–4; 22:1–5).

This broader hope is not lesser in the sense of being unreal or inferior salvation. It is the outworking of God's purpose for restored life under His kingdom. It is life granted by resurrection and sustained by divine favor. But it is described as everlasting life rather than indiscriminately as immortality. That distinction should be allowed to stand.

The righteous do not possess life by nature. They receive it by grace. Whether in the heavenly calling or in life under the kingdom on earth, all future life is God's gift through Christ. But Scripture itself distinguishes the reigning company from the broader righteous and distinguishes immortality from everlasting life. Faithful exposition must do the same.

Daniel 12 and the Two Outcomes of Resurrection

Daniel 12 remains essential because it places resurrection within the framework of final distress, divine intervention, and kingdom outcome. Michael stands up in a unique time of distress, and then "many of those sleeping in the dust of the ground will awake, these to everlasting life, but the others to reproach and everlasting contempt" (Dan. 12:1–2). The text is not concerned with intermediate conscious states. It is concerned with awakening from the dust by divine intervention.

The contrast is moral and judicial. Resurrection is not automatically blessing. It leads to divergent outcomes depending on one's standing before God. This same pattern is found in Jesus' words about resurrection to life and resurrection to judgment (John 5:28–29). The doctrine of resurrection therefore belongs to judgment as well as to hope. It magnifies Jehovah's justice as well as His mercy.

Daniel also says, "those who have insight will shine like the brightness of the expanse of heaven, and those who turn many to righteousness, like the stars forever and ever" (Dan. 12:3). This points to vindication, glory, and reward for the faithful. The resurrection is not merely restoration to prior mortal existence. It is entrance into the order appointed by God in everlasting outcome.

Death Swallowed Up in Victory

Paul brings the doctrine of resurrection to triumphant climax with the words, "When this perishable has put on the imperishable, and this mortal has put on immortality, then will come about the saying that is written, 'Death has been swallowed up in victory'" (1 Cor. 15:54). He then asks, "O death, where is your victory? O death, where is your sting?" (1 Cor. 15:55). The victory is not man's natural immortality. It is God's resurrection triumph in Christ.

Death's sting is sin, and the power of sin is the law. "But thanks be to God, who gives us the victory through our Lord Jesus Christ" (1 Cor. 15:56–57). Resurrection is therefore not a detached doctrine of future existence. It is the victory of grace over sin, of life over death, and of Christ over the curse that entered through Adam.

This victory is both already and not yet. It is already secured in Christ's resurrection. It is not yet fully applied until the dead are raised and death is abolished. That is why the church still waits. It does not wait uncertainly, but confidently. The enemy has been mortally struck in Christ's resurrection, and it will be finally abolished at the consummation of His reign.

The Resurrection and Christian Living

Paul does not end 1 Corinthians 15 with abstract theology. He ends with exhortation: "Therefore, my beloved brothers, be steadfast, immovable, always abounding in the work of the Lord, knowing that your labor is not in vain in the Lord" (1 Cor. 15:58). This is the practical force of resurrection doctrine. Because the dead are raised, Christian labor matters. Because death will be defeated, present obedience is not wasted. Because the future belongs to Christ, believers can endure suffering, loss, and persecution without despair.

The resurrection of the dead also reshapes grief. Paul says believers do not grieve as those who have no hope (1 Thess. 4:13). He does not say they do not grieve at all. Death remains grievous because it is enemy. But grief is transformed by hope because the dead in Christ will rise. Christian mourning is therefore neither stoic denial nor hopeless despair. It is sorrow tempered by the certainty of resurrection.

Resurrection also purifies faith. If the future belongs to God, then present compromises with sin are exposed as folly. If the body will be raised, then the body matters now. If death will be defeated, then allegiance to Christ is never pointless. The doctrine of resurrection therefore strengthens holiness, endurance, and faithfulness.

The Great Biblical Hope

The resurrection of the dead is the great biblical answer to death. Scripture does not teach that man survives by nature because he possesses an immortal soul. It teaches that Jehovah raises the dead through the power of Christ. The grave is real, but it is not final. Death is enemy, but it is not ultimate. Eternal life is God's gift through resurrection.

Christ has already been raised as the firstfruits. Those who belong to Him will be raised at His coming. The heavenly co-rulers receive immortality for their reign with Him. The broader righteous receive everlasting life under His kingdom. The wicked face judgment. In every case, resurrection stands as the hinge between death and everlasting outcome.

The doctrine therefore magnifies both the severity of sin and the greatness of redemption. Sin brings death. Christ conquers death. God does not merely help man endure mortality. He overthrows it. The resurrection of the dead is thus not a peripheral doctrine but one of the brightest expressions of Jehovah's saving purpose. It is the promise that the dust will not have the last word, that the dead will hear the voice of the Son, and that death itself will finally be swallowed up in victory.

Edward D. Andrews

Chapter 9 — Judgment Day: A Time of Hope

The Meaning of Judgment Day

The expression *Judgment Day* has often been misunderstood. Many imagine it as a brief moment in which all mankind is instantly sentenced, with no distinction between the overthrow of this present wicked order and the later judgment of those raised from the dead. Scripture presents the matter more carefully. The Bible does speak of a fixed day in which God will judge the inhabited earth in righteousness through Jesus Christ (Acts 17:31), but it also reveals that this judgment is administered within an ordered kingdom program centered in the thousand-year reign of Christ (Rev. 20:4–6). Judgment Day, therefore, is not best understood as a mere instant of sentencing. It is the appointed period in which the risen Christ exercises righteous rule, raises the dead according to God's purpose, opens the way for mankind to learn Jehovah's will under kingdom conditions, and brings all things to their proper moral outcome before the final abolition of death and rebellion.

This understanding immediately shows why Judgment Day is a time of hope. It is not simply the announcement of doom. It is the period in which the benefits of Christ's ransom are applied in full kingdom power. It is the era in which Satan's deception is restrained, the first-resurrection company reigns with Christ, the dead are called forth, and the nations are brought under the righteous administration of God's kingdom (Rev. 20:1–6; Isa. 11:1–10; Ps. 72:1–14). The day of judgment is therefore not the enemy of redemptive hope. It is one of its greatest expressions.

This does not lessen the severity of divine judgment. Jehovah's judgment remains real, holy, and final. The wicked present order is destroyed at the appearing of Christ. The beastly system does not continue indefinitely. The anti-God powers are judged, the lawless order is overthrown, and the present rebellion is brought to its end (2 Thess. 1:7–10; 2:8; Rev. 19:11–21). Yet that overthrow is not identical with the whole work of Judgment Day. It clears the field for it. The destruction of the wicked at Armageddon removes the present rebellious world system so that the thousand-year reign of Christ may proceed without satanic interference from the nations in the former sense (Rev. 20:1–3).

Thus the Bible requires two truths to be held together. First, Christ returns in judgment against the present anti-God order. Second, the thousand-year reign that follows is itself the great period of judgment through which the resurrected dead and surviving mankind are dealt with according to God's revealed will. When these truths are kept

Edward D. Andrews

in their proper order, the doctrine becomes clear and deeply hopeful.

The Basis for Judgment Day

Judgment Day rests upon the redemptive work of Jesus Christ. God did not appoint the world to judgment apart from first laying the basis for salvation. The whole arrangement stands upon the ransom sacrifice of His Son. Jesus declared, "God loved the world so much that He gave His only-begotten Son, in order that everyone exercising faith in Him might not be destroyed but have everlasting life" (John 3:16). His sacrificial death was not merely an example of love. It was the legal and redemptive foundation upon which restoration could be offered to fallen mankind.

From Adam onward, the human family has stood under the sentence of sin and death. Jehovah told the first man that disobedience would result in death, and when Adam sinned, he returned to the dust from which he had been taken (Gen. 2:16–17; 3:19). Scripture nowhere teaches that Adam survived death as a conscious immortal soul in another realm. Rather, the consistent testimony is that the dead are unconscious, returning to the dust, awaiting God's future act of restoration (Eccl. 9:5, 10; Ps. 146:4). "The soul that sins is the one that will die" (Ezek. 18:4), and "the wages sin pays is death" (Rom. 6:23). That sentence has passed to all because all are descendants of Adam and all have sinned (Rom. 5:12).

Judgment Day, then, is part of God's answer to the ruin brought by sin. It is not an arbitrary tribunal detached from salvation history. It is the appointed kingdom era in which the benefits of Christ's ransom are brought to bear upon mankind under righteous rule. The dead do not rise because death is unreal. They rise because Christ died and was raised. The world is judged in righteousness because the Father has appointed the Son as Judge and has furnished proof of that appointment by raising Him from the dead (Acts 17:31). Thus mercy and judgment meet in Christ. He is the Redeemer who gave His life as a ransom, and He is also the appointed Judge through whom the world will be judged.

This means that Judgment Day is not opposed to hope. It is grounded in the very act by which Jehovah opened the way for everlasting life. Men do not face a blind tribunal. They face the administration of the One who gave Himself for them. The Judge is Jesus Christ, the One who showed compassion to the suffering, who taught the truth with perfect righteousness, and who laid down His life in obedience to His Father (Matt. 11:28–30; John 5:22, 27). To be judged under such a King is not grounds for terror in itself. It is grounds for confidence in the justice, wisdom, and mercy of God.

Christ the Appointed Judge

The Scriptures place final judicial authority in the hands of the exalted Christ. Jesus said plainly, "the Father judges no one at all, but He has entrusted all the judging to the Son" (John 5:22). He also stated that the Father "gave Him authority to do judging, because He is the Son of man" (John 5:27). This is not a transfer of rule away from Jehovah, but the appointed exercise of divine judgment through the One whom Jehovah has exalted as Messiah, Lord, and King.

The apostles proclaimed this with equal clarity. Peter testified that Christ "is the one decreed by God to be judge of the living and the dead" (Acts 10:42). Paul told the Athenians that God "has set a day in which He purposes to judge the inhabited earth in righteousness by a man whom

He has appointed" (Acts 17:31). The resurrection of Jesus is the public pledge that this appointment is real and irreversible. The One who was rejected, crucified, and raised is the very One before whom all men must answer.

This gives Judgment Day a profoundly Christological character. The Judge is not an unknown force. He is the Son of God who came in humility and will return in glory. He judges as the One who knows human life from within human history, yet who remained perfectly obedient to His Father. His judgment is therefore fully righteous, uncorrupted, and exact. He is not deceived by appearances, blinded by status, or manipulated by power. He judges according to truth (Rom. 2:2, 16; Rev. 19:11).

That same reality makes Judgment Day hopeful. The One who judges is also the One through whom life comes. In John 5 Jesus joins these truths together. He speaks both of His authority to judge and of His authority to raise the dead. "The hour is coming in which all those in the memorial tombs will hear His voice and come out" (John 5:28–29). The Judge is therefore also the Life-Giver. This is essential to understanding the millennium as Judgment Day. Christ does not merely pass sentence. He reigns, raises, instructs, and administers the righteous purposes of God over mankind.

The Return of Christ and the Removal of the Present Wicked Order

Judgment Day does not begin in a vacuum. It is preceded by the visible return of Christ and the destruction of the present anti-God world order. The New Testament repeatedly teaches that Christ's appearing brings the present age of organized rebellion to its crisis and end. Jesus connected His coming with "the conclusion of the age"

(Matt. 24:3). In the explanation of the wheat and the weeds, He said that at the harvest, which is "a conclusion of a system of things," the Son of man sends forth His angels, gathers out of His kingdom all things that cause stumbling and all those doing lawlessness, and then the righteous shine forth in the kingdom of their Father (Matt. 13:39–43).

Paul describes the same crisis in 2 Thessalonians. The Lord Jesus is revealed from heaven with His powerful angels, bringing vengeance upon those who do not know God and those who do not obey the good news (2 Thess. 1:7–10). The lawless one is destroyed "by the spirit of His mouth" and "brought to nothing by the manifestation of His presence" (2 Thess. 2:8). Revelation presents the same truth symbolically and powerfully in the vision of Christ on the white horse, judging and waging war in righteousness, overthrowing the beast and the false prophet, and bringing the rebellious coalition to ruin (Rev. 19:11–21).

This destruction of the wicked at Christ's coming must not be confused with the whole work of Judgment Day. It is the necessary overthrow of the present beastly and lawless order. The old rebellious system does not continue into the millennial era. Armageddon removes it. The devil is then abyssed so that he should not deceive the nations until the thousand years are ended (Rev. 20:1–3). The kingdom reign of Christ that follows is therefore exercised under conditions radically different from the present evil world. The present order has been judged. Satan's deceiving activity over the nations in the former sense has been restrained. The thousand-year Judgment Day begins in a world no longer governed by the same beastly rebellion that marked the old age.

This is why Judgment Day is hopeful. It is not conducted in the midst of unrestrained satanic rule. It follows the overthrow of the present anti-God order.

Mankind enters that period under the authority of Christ, with the power of the beastly system broken and the deceiver bound. That is the proper setting for the resurrection, instruction, testing, and restoration that belong to the millennium.

The Resurrection of the Righteous and the Unrighteous

A central feature of Judgment Day is the resurrection of the dead. The biblical hope is not centered in the supposed immortality of the soul, but in the resurrection. Daniel 12:2 speaks of those "sleeping in the dust of the ground" who will awake, some to everlasting life and others to reproach and everlasting contempt. Jesus says that all those in the memorial tombs will hear His voice and come out, "those who did good things to a resurrection of life, those who practiced vile things to a resurrection of judgment" (John 5:28–29). Paul affirms "a resurrection both of the righteous and the unrighteous" (Acts 24:15).

This doctrine is essential to the hopefulness of Judgment Day. The dead are not beyond the reach of Jehovah's purpose. They are not abandoned in permanent unconsciousness without remedy. Christ's kingdom includes a resurrection. Those who have died are summoned forth by divine power because God has appointed His Son as both Judge and Life-Giver. The grave is real, but it is not final. Death is an enemy, but it is not invincible (1 Cor. 15:21–26).

The resurrection, however, is not flat or undifferentiated. Revelation 20:4–6 speaks first of the blessed and holy company who share in the first resurrection. These reign with Christ for a thousand years, are priests of God and of Christ, and over them the second death has no authority. This first resurrection belongs to the faithful reigning company. It marks the beginning of the millennial kingdom era and distinguishes those who share in its royal-priestly administration (Rev. 20:4–6).

The rest of the dead are then viewed in relation to the thousand-year framework. John says, "the rest of the dead did not come to life until the thousand years were ended" (Rev. 20:5). That statement preserves the distinction between the first-resurrection company and the broader dealings with the dead in the millennial and post-millennial sequence. The wider biblical witness still stands clearly: there is a resurrection of the righteous and the unrighteous (Acts 24:15), and Christ's voice reaches all in the tombs (John 5:28–29). Judgment Day therefore includes not only the reign of the first-resurrection company with Christ, but also the broader kingdom process by which the dead are brought forward under divine judgment.

This is a time of hope because resurrection means that death does not have the final word. The righteous are not forgotten, and even the unrighteous are not simply ignored as though Jehovah's justice and mercy had no ordered dealing with them. The resurrection itself is already a testimony that God's purpose in Christ extends beyond the grave.

The Books Were Opened

John's vision of the great white throne says that "scrolls were opened, and another scroll was opened; it is the scroll of life. And the dead were judged out of those things written in the scrolls according to their deeds" (Rev. 20:12). This imagery is often treated only as the scene of final sentencing, but within the broader biblical framework it also points to the ordered, revealed basis on which judgment proceeds. God does not judge in arbitrariness. He judges in truth, according to what He has made known.

The opening of the scrolls evidently signifies the full disclosure of divine standards, divine record, and divine requirements in relation to those being judged. Nothing is forgotten, hidden, or confused before the throne of God. Yet this imagery also fits the millennial administration of Judgment Day. Christ's reign is not an empty suspension between the destruction of the old world and the final state. It is a kingdom era marked by rule, judgment, priestly service, and ordered administration (Rev. 20:4–6). In that setting, the opening of the scrolls corresponds well with the progressive revealing and application of God's righteous requirements under the reign of Christ.

This accords with the broader pattern of Scripture. Men are judged according to their response to divine revelation. Jesus said, "the word that I have spoken is what will judge him in the last day" (John 12:48). Paul says that God "will render to each one according to his works" (Rom. 2:6), not because works earn life apart from grace, but because deeds reveal loyalty, faith, rebellion, or lawlessness. The judgment is moral, covenantal, and truthful. It reveals what a person loved, obeyed, and served.

During the millennial Judgment Day, therefore, those under Christ's rule are not left in ignorance. Judgment is not blind doom. It is government by revealed righteousness. The opening of the scrolls points to that reality. Those who respond obediently to Jehovah's standards under the reign of Christ show themselves aligned with life. Those who refuse reveal that they remain opposed to God even under righteous kingdom conditions. In that sense the books are opened not merely to expose the past, but to establish the divine standard by which mankind is judged within the kingdom administration of Christ.

This makes Judgment Day a time of hope because it is not a chaotic moment of terror. It is a righteous and ordered administration under the Messiah, in which the truth of God is made plain and men are judged according to that truth.

The Nations Under Christ's Judgment

The millennium is not a detached heavenly abstraction with no relation to the earth. Revelation 20 says that Satan is bound "so that he should not mislead the nations any longer until the thousand years were ended" (Rev. 20:3). That statement implies the continued existence of nations during the thousand years and shows that the reign of Christ has direct significance for the human order. The point is not merely that Satan is personally restrained. The point is that the conditions of human life are changed under the kingdom rule of Christ.

This fits the wider prophetic hope. Psalm 72 describes the king ruling from sea to sea, defending the lowly, delivering the needy, and bringing blessing to the nations (Ps. 72:1–14). Isaiah 11 describes the reign of the shoot from Jesse as an era in which righteousness marks His rule, the earth is filled with the knowledge of Jehovah, and the nations are ordered under Him (Isa. 11:1–10). Zechariah speaks of Jehovah becoming King over all the earth (Zech. 14:9). These passages show that kingdom rule extends to the human realm and is directed toward restoration and righteous order.

Thus Judgment Day is not merely about condemnation. It is about the exercise of righteous dominion over mankind. Christ's thousand-year reign serves the restoration process by which His authority is openly exercised over the realm once dominated by sin, deception, and beastly rebellion. Those who survive the overthrow of the wicked order enter this new phase not to drift in moral uncertainty, but to live under the direct administration of divine righteousness. The same is true of those who are raised under Christ's kingdom purpose. Judgment Day is therefore a time of kingdom order, not a moment of blind destruction.

This explains why the doctrine belongs to hope. The nations are not abandoned. The earth is not discarded. God's purpose is not merely to remove a select company to heaven while leaving the earth forever under the shadow of Adam's fall. The thousand-year reign is part of the great restoration movement by which Christ's rule is brought to bear upon the human scene in preparation for the final renewal.

The Final Test After the Thousand Years

Judgment Day does not terminate in vague sentiment or automatic universal success. Revelation 20 shows that after the thousand years Satan is released for a short time, deceives the nations once more, and gathers them for a final rebellion commonly associated with Gog and Magog (Rev. 20:7–9). This final release is not a contradiction of kingdom hope. It is part of the ordered wisdom of God. It exposes once and for all the moral state of those who stand under the kingdom after the thousand-year reign.

The release proves that judgment is not superficial. It is not merely external conformity under ideal conditions. The final test reveals whether those who have lived under Christ's righteous rule truly stand in loyal obedience to God or whether rebellion still lies hidden within. Fire comes down from heaven and devours the rebels, and the devil who deceived them is thrown into the lake of fire, where his judgment is complete and irreversible (Rev. 20:9–10).

This final testing helps clarify the meaning of Judgment Day as a time of hope. Hope is not sentimental optimism. It is hope grounded in the certainty that Jehovah's purpose will fully succeed. Evil will not be left unexposed. Rebellion will not survive hidden beneath outward order. The thousand-year reign brings mankind to the point at which a final moral division is publicly revealed. Those who remain loyal enter the everlasting blessing of God's completed purpose. Those who rebel are removed. Divine justice is therefore not partial or unfinished. It is brought to completion.

The final release of Satan also confirms that the millennium is a transitional kingdom era rather than the ultimate state itself. Death has not yet been finally abolished. The last rebellion still lies ahead. The great white throne still follows. The new heaven and new earth still await. Judgment Day is therefore the great kingdom period moving history toward its final moral and redemptive outcome.

The Great White Throne and the Second Death

After the thousand years and the final rebellion, John sees the great white throne (Rev. 20:11–15). The throne is great because its authority is supreme and final. It is white because the judgment issuing from it is pure, holy, and uncorrupted. Earth and heaven flee from before it because the old order, marked by death, rebellion, and curse, has no continuing place before the final judgment of God (Rev. 20:11).

The dead, the great and the small, stand before the throne. The sea gives up the dead in it, and death and Hades give up the dead in them. All are judged according to their deeds (Rev. 20:12–13). The language is universal and exact. No human rank matters here. No realm of death can conceal the dead from divine summons. Judgment is complete, public, and morally precise.

Then comes one of the most decisive interpretive statements in the chapter: "death and Hades were hurled into the lake of fire. This means the second death, the lake of fire" (Rev. 20:14). Scripture here defines its own symbolism. The lake of fire is the second death. It is not presented as a place where the wicked are preserved eternally in conscious torment as though eternal life were granted to them in another form. Rather, it is final, irreversible destruction. Death remains death, even when it is final. Eternal life is the gift of God to the saved, not the possession of the wicked in endless suffering (John 3:16; Rom. 6:23).

This agrees with the wider testimony of Scripture. Jesus says God can destroy both soul and body in Gehenna (Matt. 10:28). Paul speaks of "everlasting destruction" from the presence of the Lord (2 Thess. 1:9). Revelation calls the final punishment "the second death" (Rev. 20:14; 21:8). Punishment is eternal in result because it is irreversible, not because the condemned are immortalized in pain. Evil is removed, not preserved forever as an everlasting rival realm within God's creation.

This, too, is part of why Judgment Day is a time of hope. It means evil does not endure forever. Death itself is thrown into the lake of fire. Hades is abolished. Rebellion reaches its end. Jehovah's purpose is not to preserve sin, Satan, and the wicked as an eternal counter-kingdom. It is to remove them completely so that righteousness may dwell without rival.

A Time of Hope

Judgment Day is rightly called a time of hope because it is inseparable from resurrection, kingdom rule, restoration, and the final triumph of righteousness. It is the period in which Christ openly exercises the authority given Him by the Father. It is the era in which the first-resurrection company reigns with Him, the nations are brought under righteous rule, the dead are dealt with according to God's purpose, and the whole human scene is moved toward its final moral outcome (Rev. 20:4–6; Acts 24:15; John 5:28–29).

It is hopeful because the dead are not forgotten. There is a resurrection of both the righteous and the unrighteous. It is hopeful because the world is not left forever under Satan's deception. He is bound for the thousand years. It is hopeful because the old beastly order is not eternal. It is destroyed at Christ's appearing. It is hopeful because the opening of the books means mankind is judged under revealed righteousness, not abandoned to confusion. It is hopeful because the second death removes evil finally and completely. It is hopeful because death itself is abolished, and God's purpose moves openly toward the new heaven and the new earth in which righteousness dwells (Rev. 21:1–4; 1 Cor. 15:24–28; 2 Pet. 3:13).

This is why Scripture can speak of divine judgment in ways that summon rejoicing rather than despair. The psalmist says, "Let the heavens rejoice, and let the earth be joyful; let the sea thunder and that which fills it. Let the open field exult and all that is in it. At the same time let all the trees of the forest break out joyfully before Jehovah. For He has come; for He has come to judge the earth. He will judge the inhabited earth with righteousness and the peoples with His faithfulness" (Ps. 96:11–13). Judgment is joyful there because it means the end of oppression, the vindication of righteousness, and the open triumph of Jehovah's rule.

Thus Judgment Day is not to be feared as though it were the triumph of arbitrary severity. It is the ordered, righteous, and hopeful reign of Christ in which the effects of His ransom are brought to bear upon mankind, rebellion is fully exposed, the faithful are vindicated, and the whole creation moves toward the final removal of death and evil. It is a time of hope because it is one of the greatest expressions of Jehovah's justice, mercy, and kingdom purpose in Christ.

Chapter 10 — The Destruction of the Antichristic Order

The Collapse of the Anti-God Order

The return of Jesus Christ does not merely comfort the faithful and vindicate the righteous. It also brings the antichristic order to its appointed end. Scripture does not portray evil as slowly fading away through moral progress, political reform, or religious influence. It portrays evil as maturing into an anti-God system of deception, false worship, lawlessness, and beastly power, and then being overthrown by the appearing of Christ. The final victory belongs neither to the lawless one nor to the beast, neither to the false prophet nor to the dragon who empowers them.

Edward D. Andrews

It belongs to the Son of God, whose return is decisive, public, and irreversible.

This truth is essential because biblical prophecy does not end in tension. It moves toward resolution. The apostasy comes. The man of lawlessness is revealed. The beastly order rises. The false prophet deceives. The nations are gathered in rebellion. But none of these realities is ultimate. They are permitted for a time, exposed by the Word of God, and then judged by the returning Christ. The whole anti-God order that opposes Jehovah and His Anointed is brought down in one climactic intervention of divine justice.

This overthrow is not merely political. It is theological and judicial. The final enemy system is destroyed because it blasphemes God, persecutes the holy ones, demands worship, and exalts itself against the truth. The victory of Christ is therefore not only the defeat of hostile powers. It is the restoration of rightful order in the universe. False worship is ended. beastly dominion is shattered. The lie is exposed. The saints are vindicated. The kingdom of God advances openly.

The Lawless One Destroyed by the Appearing of Christ

Paul states the destruction of the antichristic order with exceptional clarity in 2 Thessalonians 2. After describing the apostasy and the revelation of the man of lawlessness, he declares: "Then that lawless one will be revealed, whom the Lord Jesus will slay with the breath of His mouth and bring to nothing by the appearance of His coming" (2 Thess. 2:8). This statement is one of the clearest summaries in all Scripture of the fate of final rebellion.

142

The man of lawlessness is allowed to emerge. He opposes and exalts himself above every so-called god or object of worship. He installs himself in the place that belongs to God and publicly displays himself as divine (2 Thess. 2:3–4). His coming is according to the working of Satan, with power, signs, and lying wonders (2 Thess. 2:9). He deceives those who do not love the truth (2 Thess. 2:10–12). But Paul does not linger on his rise without immediately declaring his end. The lawless one is not a permanent mystery. He is a doomed usurper.

Paul says Christ will slay him "with the breath of His mouth." This language recalls Isaiah 11:4, where the Messianic ruler strikes the earth with the rod of His mouth and slays the wicked with the breath of His lips. The point is not that Christ requires military struggle in the ordinary sense. The point is His sovereign judicial authority. His word is enough. The same mouth that spoke creation into being and spoke truth into the world will speak judgment upon the lawless one. The rebellion that appears so imposing in history is ended by the authority of the King.

Paul also says the lawless one will be brought to nothing "by the appearance of His coming." The term emphasizes manifestation, splendor, open revelation. Christ's victory is therefore not hidden, gradual, or symbolic. It is achieved by His appearing. The lawless one cannot survive the unveiled presence of the Lord. The anti-God order may flourish in darkness and deception, but it collapses when confronted by the visible glory of Christ.

This means the return of Jesus is itself the destruction of the lawless rebellion. The final anti-God structure does not outlast His appearing. It is not negotiated with, reformed, or slowly absorbed. It is ended.

Revelation 19 and the Overthrow of the Beast

Revelation 19 expands this same truth in apocalyptic imagery. John sees heaven opened and the rider on the white horse appearing in majesty: "the one seated on it is called Faithful and True, and in righteousness He judges and wages war" (Rev. 19:11). His eyes are a flame of fire. On His head are many diadems. He is clothed in an outer garment dipped in blood. His name is called The Word of God. He comes with the armies of heaven, and on His garment and on His thigh a name is written: "King of kings and Lord of lords" (Rev. 19:12–16). Every feature of the vision proclaims authority, righteousness, and irresistible kingship.

The context makes clear that this is the return of Christ in judicial power. The beast and the kings of the earth gather their armies "to wage war against the one seated on the horse and against His army" (Rev. 19:19). The anti-God coalition reaches its climax. The rebellious powers of the earth are no longer merely opposed to God in principle. They are gathered in open defiance of the returning King. This is the highest expression of antichristic rebellion: creaturely power organized against Christ Himself.

Yet the battle is not described as prolonged or uncertain. John does not narrate an extended struggle because the outcome is never in doubt. "The beast was taken, and with him the false prophet that performed the signs in his sight" (Rev. 19:20). The one who seemed invincible is seized. The one who deceived the nations with signs is seized . The anti-God political-religious order, so terrifying in Revelation 13, is dismantled immediately before the appearing of Christ.

The false prophet is specifically identified as the one "who deceived those who had received the mark of the beast and those who worshiped his image" (Rev. 19:20). This reminds the reader that the final conflict was always about worship and truth. The beast demanded allegiance. The false prophet sacralized that demand. The image enforced it. The mark identified those who yielded to it. When Christ returns, all of that machinery of deception is exposed and destroyed. The whole system that claimed ultimate loyalty is judged by the One to whom all loyalty actually belongs.

John then says, "these two were thrown alive into the lake of fire that burns with sulfur" (Rev. 19:20). The beast and the false prophet are not rehabilitated. They are not left in place under a new arrangement. They are removed in final judgment. The rest of the rebellious host are slain by the sword proceeding from the mouth of the rider (Rev. 19:21). Once again, Christ judges by His word. His sovereign speech brings the rebellion to its end.

The Beastly Powers and False Religion Brought Down Together

One of the most important features of the final judgment is that the beast and the false prophet fall together. Scripture does not present the final anti-God system as merely political tyranny. It is political-religious totality. The beast from the sea represents the final anti-God dominion in its imperial and blasphemous form (Rev. 13:1–10). The beast from the earth, later called the false prophet, represents the deceptive religious power that causes the world to worship the beast, receive his mark, and submit to his image (Rev. 13:11–18; 19:20).

Edward D. Andrews

This union of political force and false religion is central to the character of the antichristic order. The beast does not rest content with administration. He requires worship. The false prophet does not merely preach spirituality. He sanctifies rebellion. Together they form a total order of coercion, propaganda, false signs, and idolatry. The final rebellion is therefore not only a matter of oppressive rule. It is a counterfeit kingdom demanding the devotion that belongs to God.

At Christ's return, that union is broken forever. The beast is seized. The false prophet is seized. The system of power and deception that they represent is ended. Revelation does not permit the reader to imagine that false religion and beastly politics will somehow survive under Christ's manifest rule. They are judged together because they worked together against God.

This shows the comprehensiveness of Christ's victory. He does not merely defeat open violence while leaving deception untouched. He destroys both coercion and falsehood, both imperial arrogance and counterfeit spirituality, both the sword and the lie. The antichristic order falls in all its dimensions.

Satan's Influence Broken at Christ's Return

Although the final destruction of Satan is described later in Revelation 20:10, his influence over the nations is broken decisively in connection with Christ's victory over the beastly order. Revelation 20 follows directly after Revelation 19: the beast and false prophet are judged, then Satan is bound, thrown into the abyss, and shut in "so that he should deceive the nations no longer until the thousand years were finished" (Rev. 20:1–3). This sequence is vital.

Satan is the source of the beast's authority (Rev. 13:2). He is the dragon behind the whole anti-God structure (Rev. 12:9, 17). His war against the holy ones takes historical form through the beast, the false prophet, and the kings of the earth. Therefore, when Christ destroys the beastly coalition, He also strips Satan of his operative rule over the nations in that final form. The dragon's earthly machinery collapses. His power to deceive in the same open and global way is interrupted by divine judgment. He is bound.

This binding is not yet his final destruction, but it is the decisive end of his beastly regime. The antichristic order cannot rise again after Christ appears. The dragon who empowered it is restrained, imprisoned, and rendered unable to continue deceiving the nations in the same fashion. This means the victory of Christ is not temporary or reversible. The system of satanic deception that dominated the final rebellion is ended when the King returns and Satan is bound under divine authority.

That distinction should be maintained carefully. The beast and false prophet are destroyed at Christ's return. Satan's final destruction comes after the thousand years and after the final release and rebellion described in Revelation 20:7–10. But his antichristic influence through the beastly order is decisively broken at Christ's appearing. The world-system he energized is shattered, and he is confined so that its global deception cannot continue.

Christ's Victory Is Decisive

Scripture emphasizes the decisiveness of Christ's victory in several ways. First, the enemies are seized, not merely weakened. The beast is taken. The false prophet is taken. The rebellious armies are slain. Satan is bound. The anti-God order is not left partially intact, waiting to regain strength immediately. It is dismantled by divine judgment.

Second, the victory is judicial and public. Christ does not win by secret influence or hidden spiritual process. He appears, judges, wages war in righteousness, and destroys the rebellion before all creation. The victory is therefore a manifestation of truth. The world that admired the beast must now see the beast exposed. The nations that followed false signs must now see the false prophet judged. The kings that boasted against heaven must now stand before the King of kings.

Third, the victory is morally final. The antichristic order does not merely suffer defeat in battle. It receives sentence. The beast and false prophet are cast into the lake of fire. The rebellion is judged because it is wicked, false, and blasphemous. Christ's victory is not only power over power. It is righteousness over evil.

Fourth, the victory is covenantal. The holy ones whom the beast persecuted are vindicated. Those who refused the mark and did not worship the image are shown to have stood on the side of truth (Rev. 20:4). The final conflict was always about allegiance, and Christ's victory publicly reveals the righteousness of those who remained faithful to Him.

Christ's Victory Is Irreversible

The destruction of the antichristic order is not only decisive. It is irreversible. Scripture does not present the beast and false prophet as later reemerging. Their judgment is final. They are thrown into the lake of fire at Christ's return (Rev. 19:20), and later, when Satan himself is cast into the lake of fire, he is cast "where the beast and the false prophet are also" (Rev. 20:10). The final anti-God political-religious order is therefore not cyclical. It is ended permanently.

This irreversible character is essential to biblical hope. If the beastly order could return again and again in the same final sense, then Christ's appearing would not be the true end of the antichristic system. But Scripture will not permit that thought. The return of Christ brings a real conclusion. The beast does not recover. The false prophet does not regroup. The mark of the beast does not remain a viable structure of allegiance. The image does not stand. The lawless one is not merely embarrassed. He is destroyed.

Satan's later release at the end of the thousand years does not change this. Revelation 20 describes a final rebellion under his direct deception after his release, not a restoration of the former beastly regime. The beast and false prophet are already judged. The antichristic order of Revelation 13 and 19 is finished. The last rebellion that follows later is also crushed, and then Satan himself is finally destroyed in the lake of fire (Rev. 20:7–10). Thus the victory of Christ unfolds in ordered stages, but each stage is irreversible. What Christ judges does not return as though His judgment had failed.

The End of False Worship

Because the antichristic order is fundamentally about false worship, its destruction means the end of that counterfeit claim upon humanity. The beast demanded worship. The false prophet enforced it. The image embodied it. The mark signified it. The kings of the earth supported it. In all of this, the central issue was whether creation would render allegiance to the dragon's order or to God and the Lamb.

When Christ returns, that false worship is exposed as fraud. The beast is not divine. The false prophet is not holy. The image has no life before the living God. The mark confers no safety. The kings of the earth are not ultimate. The dragon is not sovereign. The whole system is laid bare for what it always was: rebellion masquerading as glory, idolatry dressed as order, blasphemy claiming sacred authority.

This is why the judgment of the antichristic order is also a vindication of the first commandment. Jehovah alone is God. The Lamb alone is worthy. The destruction of the beastly order restores the created order to truth by removing the power that sought to redirect worship away from God.

The Comfort of the Faithful

The destruction of the antichristic order is not merely a warning to the wicked. It is a comfort to the faithful. The holy ones are called to endure because the beast's triumph is temporary (Rev. 13:10; 14:12). They are called to reject the mark because Christ will judge those who receive it and vindicate those who refuse it (Rev. 14:9–12; 20:4). They are called to suffer faithfully because the King is coming.

This means the church need not fear as though the final anti-God system might somehow win. It may appear dominant for a time. It may deceive many. It may coerce through politics, religion, and economics. It may wage war against the holy ones. But it cannot survive the appearing of Christ. The faithful therefore endure, not because evil is weak, but because Christ is stronger. They refuse false worship because the Lamb will triumph. They remain loyal because the beast is doomed.

The destruction of the antichristic order also assures believers that history is not trapped in endless cycles of oppression. The final rebellion has an appointed limit. God has not abandoned the world to the dragon. The same Scriptures that foretell the rise of lawlessness also foretell its destruction. The same Lord who warned of false christs and false prophets also promised to come in power and great glory. The same Revelation that unveils the beast also unveils his doom.

The Irresistible Triumph of the King

The destruction of the antichristic order reveals the irresistible triumph of Jesus Christ. He returns as the Judge, the Warrior, the Word of God, and the King of kings. He slays the lawless one with the breath of His mouth. He seizes the beast and false prophet. He destroys the rebellious coalition. He breaks Satan's influence over the nations by binding the dragon. He ends the final anti-God political-religious system forever.

This victory is not partial. It is not symbolic. It is not reversible. It is the decisive intervention by which the false kingdom collapses before the true King. The rebellion of man energized by Satan reaches its climax only to be shattered by the appearing of Christ. The victory is judicial, public, moral, and final.

For that reason, the church does not look to the future with dread as though the last word belongs to the beast. It looks to the future with sober confidence, knowing that the King will appear, the antichristic order will fall, and every rival claim to worship and rule will be brought to nothing. Christ's victory is decisive. Christ's victory is irreversible. Christ's victory is the end of the anti-God system and the open beginning of His righteous reign.

Chapter 11 — The Millennial Reign of Christ

The Thousand Years in the Purpose of God

The millennial reign of Christ is one of the clearest and most important parts of biblical prophecy. Scripture does not present it as a vague symbol of the present church age, nor as a poetic way of describing moral progress in history. It presents it as a real and ordered phase in the kingdom purpose of God. Revelation 20 speaks explicitly of a thousand years during which Satan is bound, the blessed and holy share in the first resurrection, and they reign with Christ as priests and kings under His authority (Rev. 20:1–6). This reign stands after the visible return of Christ in Revelation 19 and before the final release of Satan, the last rebellion, the great white throne, and the new heaven and new earth (Rev. 19:11–21; 20:1–15; 21:1).

That sequence matters. Revelation 19 shows Christ appearing openly in glory, judging and waging war in righteousness, destroying the beast and the false prophet, and overthrowing the anti-God coalition (Rev. 19:11–21). Revelation 20 then moves to the binding of Satan and the thousand-year reign (Rev. 20:1–6). Only after the thousand years are completed does Satan go out again to deceive the nations, lead a final rebellion, and meet his end before the last judgment (Rev. 20:7–15). The order is deliberate. Christ returns before the thousand years. For that reason, the biblical doctrine is premillennial.

This must be stated plainly because the kingdom of God unfolds in the order Scripture gives. Christ does not return after the thousand years. He returns before them, inaugurates them, and reigns through them. The millennium is therefore not an optional appendix to prophecy. It is a revealed kingdom phase in which Christ administers His victory over the nations, vindicates His faithful ones, restrains satanic deception, and advances the divine purpose toward final restoration.

Revelation 20 and the Order of Events

Revelation 20 opens with John seeing an angel coming down from heaven with the key of the abyss and a great chain in his hand (Rev. 20:1). He seizes "the dragon, the original serpent, who is the Devil and Satan," binds him for a thousand years, throws him into the abyss, and shuts and seals it over him "so that he would not deceive the nations any longer until the thousand years were ended" (Rev. 20:2–3). The language is direct. Satan is bound. The purpose of the binding is stated. The duration is stated. The nations are no longer deceived in the same way during that period.

This binding follows the destruction of the beast and false prophet in Revelation 19. The sequence cannot be ignored. It does not describe the present age, in which Satan is still called "the god of this system of things" and the whole world is lying in the power of the wicked one (2 Cor. 4:4; 1 John 5:19). Nor does it describe an age in which the beastly order continues to dominate the world. It follows Christ's visible victory over the anti-God system. The dragon who empowered the beast is therefore restrained after Christ appears in judgment.

John then sees thrones and those seated upon them, and authority to judge is given to them. He also sees those who had been faithful under beastly persecution, those who had not worshiped the beast or its image and had not received its mark upon their forehead or hand. "They came to life and ruled as kings with the Christ for the thousand years" (Rev. 20:4). John calls this "the first resurrection" (Rev. 20:5). He adds, "Happy and holy is anyone having part in the first resurrection; over these the second death has no authority, but they will be priests of God and of the Christ, and they will rule as kings with Him for the thousand years" (Rev. 20:6).

These verses establish a definite kingdom order. Satan is bound. The first-resurrection company reigns with Christ. The second death has no authority over them. Their reign is royal and priestly. Its duration is a thousand years. Nothing in the passage suggests that the thousand years are merely a symbolic description of the present age between Christ's first and second comings. The sequence belongs after the defeat of the beast, not before it.

The Premillennial Nature of the Kingdom

Premillennialism is not an artificial theological construction forced onto Scripture. It arises from the plain order of Revelation itself. Christ appears in chapter 19. Satan is bound and the thousand-year reign begins in chapter 20. After the thousand years, Satan is released, deceives the nations again, and gathers them for final rebellion. That rebellion is destroyed. Then comes the great white throne and, after that, the new heaven and new earth (Rev. 20:7–21:1).

If Christ returned after the millennium, the order of Revelation 19–20 would be profoundly misleading. But the text is not misleading. It is orderly. The beast and false prophet are judged first. Satan is then bound. The first-resurrection company reigns. Satan is later released and finally destroyed. The dead are judged. The new creation follows. The premillennial reading is therefore not speculative system-building. It is the most natural reading of the passage as it stands.

This also harmonizes with the broader biblical witness. Daniel 7 presents the destruction of beastly dominion and the giving of kingdom authority to the Son of Man and to the holy ones (Dan. 7:11–14, 18, 27). First Corinthians 15 says that Christ must reign until He has put all enemies under His feet, and the last enemy to be abolished is death (1 Cor. 15:23–26). Revelation 20 gives the kingdom phase within that broader process. Christ returns, the holy ones reign with Him, Satan's deceiving activity over the nations is restrained, and the divine purpose moves forward until every enemy is abolished.

Thus the millennium is neither a substitute for Christ's return nor an age that precedes it. It is the kingdom period that begins because He has returned.

The First Resurrection and the Reigning Company

The first resurrection stands at the center of the millennial reign. John says plainly, "This is the first resurrection" (Rev. 20:5). Those who share in it are blessed and holy. They reign with Christ. Over them the second death has no authority (Rev. 20:6). This first resurrection identifies the reigning company and clarifies the nature of their reward.

These participants are described as those who remained faithful in the face of beastly oppression. They did not worship the beast or its image and did not receive its mark (Rev. 20:4). Their loyalty under pressure leads to vindicated participation in Christ's reign. They are priests of God and of Christ, language that communicates consecrated service as well as royal authority (Rev. 20:6).

This company is most directly associated with immortality in the full Pauline sense. Paul speaks of mortality putting on immortality and corruption putting on incorruption (1 Cor. 15:53–54). Revelation says the second death has no authority over those in the first resurrection (Rev. 20:6). These truths fit together. The first-resurrection company is not merely granted unending life in general terms. It is raised to reign with Christ in royal-priestly service.

That distinction should be preserved. Scripture does not describe every future aspect of life in identical terms. There is the first resurrection, and it belongs to a blessed and holy company who reign with Christ for the thousand years (Rev. 20:4–6). There is also a resurrection of both the righteous and the unrighteous more broadly (Acts 24:15), and Christ says all those in the memorial tombs will hear His voice and come out, some to a resurrection of life and others to a resurrection of judgment (John 5:28–29). The first resurrection is therefore distinguished within the larger framework of resurrection and judgment. It identifies the reigning company through whom Christ administers His kingdom during the millennial age.

Judgment Day and the Thousand Years

The thousand-year reign is also the proper setting for understanding Judgment Day. Scripture does speak of a fixed day in which God will judge the inhabited earth in righteousness through Jesus Christ (Acts 17:31). Yet the judgment of mankind is not exhausted in the single act by which Christ destroys the present wicked order at His appearing. Armageddon brings the present rebellious world system to its end, but the thousand years that follow are the period in which Christ administers righteous judgment over mankind under kingdom conditions (Rev. 19:11–21; 20:1–6).

This is why Judgment Day is rightly understood as the thousand-year reign of Christ. It is during that era that Satan is restrained, the first-resurrection company reigns, and the divine standards are brought to bear upon mankind under the righteous administration of the Messiah. Revelation 20 speaks of books being opened and the dead being judged according to the things written in those books (Rev. 20:12). This fits the millennial setting. Judgment is not blind doom.

It is righteous administration according to revealed standards.

The resurrection of the righteous and the unrighteous belongs to that hope. Paul expressly taught "a resurrection both of the righteous and the unrighteous" (Acts 24:15). Jesus said all those in the memorial tombs would hear His voice and come out (John 5:28–29). Judgment Day is therefore a time of hope because the dead are not forgotten. The reign of Christ includes resurrection and judgment in a kingdom framework that serves Jehovah's righteous and merciful purpose.

The Thousand Years Are Not the Present Age

Many interpreters have treated the thousand years as symbolic of the present church age. Yet this reading does not fit the details of Revelation 20. The passage says Satan is bound so that he might not deceive the nations any longer until the thousand years are ended (Rev. 20:3). That does not match the present age, in which deception still dominates the nations and the dragon continues his war against the truth (Rev. 12:9, 17; 13:2, 7, 14).

Nor does the present age fit the scene of Revelation 20:4–6. The first resurrection is connected with reigning with Christ for a thousand years after the defeat of the beast. The participants are those vindicated after refusing the mark of the beast. This belongs after the final anti-God conflict, not before it. The later release of Satan also resists identification of the thousand years with the present age. After the thousand years are completed, Satan is released for a short time, deceives the nations again, gathers them for rebellion, and is then destroyed (Rev. 20:7–10). If the thousand years were merely the present age, this later release would become unintelligible or uncontrolled symbolism.

The thousand years therefore function as a real kingdom period within the final administration of God's purpose. The number itself may carry the sense of divine completeness and appointed fullness, yet the reign it describes is no less real for that reason. The text does not invite the interpreter to dissolve the millennium into a general symbol for the present age.

The Purpose of the Millennial Reign

The millennial reign has a necessary purpose in the outworking of God's kingdom. It is not an unnecessary pause between Christ's return and the final state. It is the divinely ordered phase through which Christ openly administers His victory, vindicates His faithful ones, judges mankind under righteous standards, restrains satanic deception, and moves history toward complete restoration.

First, the millennium manifests Christ's kingly authority over the world that rebelled against Him. Psalm 2 promised that the nations would be given to the Son and that He would shepherd them with a rod of iron (Ps. 2:8–9). Revelation applies that authority to Christ and, in subordinate participation, to His faithful ones (Rev. 2:26–27; 12:5; 19:15). The thousand years are therefore one important sphere in which Messianic dominion is openly exercised.

Second, the millennium vindicates the holy ones. Those who suffered under the beast do not merely survive in memory. They reign with Christ. The world that despised them sees the reversal of God's judgment. This fulfills Daniel's promise that "the holy ones of the Supreme One will receive the kingdom" (Dan. 7:18, 27).

Third, the millennium restrains Satan's deception among the nations. Satan is not yet finally destroyed at the beginning of the thousand years, but he is bound so that he cannot deceive the nations in the same way (Rev. 20:2–3). This marks the millennial kingdom as an era of radically altered conditions in relation to the dragon's former dominance.

Fourth, the millennium belongs to the ordered defeat of all enemies until death itself is abolished. Paul says Christ must reign until all enemies are placed under His feet, and "as the last enemy, death is to be brought to nothing" (1 Cor. 15:25–26). Revelation 20 situates that reign within the final stages of history. The thousand years lead toward the point at which death and Hades are finally thrown into the lake of fire (Rev. 20:14).

The Reigning Faithful and the Kingdom Administration

Those who reign with Christ during the millennium are not passive spectators. Revelation says they "ruled as kings with the Christ for the thousand years" and that they are "priests of God and of the Christ" (Rev. 20:4, 6). Their role is therefore royal and priestly. The heavenly calling is not mere privilege without function. It is participation in kingdom administration under the authority of the Messiah.

This is consistent with the wider New Testament witness. Jesus promised the little flock the kingdom (Luke 12:32). He told His faithful apostles that they would sit on thrones (Luke 22:28–30). Paul asks, "Do you not know that the holy ones will judge the world?" (1 Cor. 6:2). Revelation 5:9–10 speaks of those purchased by the Lamb as a kingdom and priests. These passages together show that the faithful heavenly company shares in Christ's royal administration.

That reign is always derivative, never equal to Christ's own kingship. Christ remains the King. The faithful reign with Him, not apart from Him. Their authority is granted, subordinate, priestly, and real. The millennial reign therefore displays the generosity of Jehovah's kingdom purpose. The faithful are not only spared judgment. They are exalted into service under Christ and given a role in His righteous administration.

The Nations Under Christ's Reign

Revelation 20 does not describe every detail of life among the nations during the thousand years, but it clearly implies their existence by saying that Satan is bound so that he should not deceive the nations any longer until the thousand years are completed (Rev. 20:3). This means the millennial reign is not an abstract heavenly condition detached from the earth. It has direct significance for the nations and for human life under kingdom rule.

This agrees with the broader prophetic hope. Psalm 72 describes the king ruling from sea to sea, judging the afflicted, delivering the poor, and bringing blessing to the nations (Ps. 72:1–14). Isaiah 11 speaks of the root of Jesse ruling in righteousness, the earth being filled with the knowledge of Jehovah, and the nations looking to Him (Isa. 11:1–10). Zechariah 14 declares that Jehovah will become King over all the earth (Zech. 14:9). The millennial reign belongs to that larger biblical expectation of righteous dominion extended over the human order.

This also helps preserve the full scope of God's purpose. The kingdom is not exhausted in heavenly blessedness alone. Jehovah's purpose is not merely to take a select company to heaven while abandoning His larger purpose for the earth. The thousand-year reign serves the

Edward D. Andrews

restoration process by which Christ's rule is openly exercised over the realm previously dominated by beastly rebellion and satanic deception, moving all things toward the final renewal in which righteousness fully dwells.

The Final Release of Satan

After the thousand years are completed, Satan is released from his prison for a short time (Rev. 20:7). This release does not weaken the doctrine of the millennium. It completes its moral purpose. Satan goes out once more "to mislead those nations in the four corners of the earth, Gog and Magog," and gathers them for battle (Rev. 20:8). Their number is like the sand of the sea. They come over the breadth of the earth and surround the camp of the holy ones and the beloved city, but fire comes down from heaven and devours them (Rev. 20:9).

This final rebellion shows that evil is not merely the product of bad external conditions. Even after a thousand years of Christ's righteous rule and Satan's restraint, rebellion reveals itself again when the deceiver is released. The release therefore exposes the moral state of those who refuse steadfast loyalty to God. It vindicates divine justice by showing that the final destruction of rebellion is not arbitrary. Evil remains evil and manifests itself when given the opportunity.

Then the devil who deceived them is hurled into the lake of fire (Rev. 20:10). The dragon who stood behind the beastly system, the false prophet, and the war against the holy ones finally meets his end. The millennium therefore leads directly into the complete removal of satanic opposition and the final moral cleansing of God's creation.

The Millennium and Final Restoration

The thousand-year reign must be seen in relation to God's final restoration. It is not the ultimate state, but it is ordered toward it. Revelation 20 does not end with the millennium. After the thousand years come the final rebellion, the destruction of Satan, the great white throne, the judgment of the dead, the abolition of death and Hades, and then the new heaven and new earth (Rev. 20:7–21:1).

This shows that the millennium is not itself the final perfected state. Death still remains to be abolished in its last expression. Satan still exists until his final destruction after the thousand years. The great white throne still lies ahead. The new heaven and new earth still await. The millennium is therefore a transitional kingdom era within God's final program. It is indispensable, but it is not ultimate.

Its purpose in relation to restoration is profound. It displays Christ's righteous reign before the final abolition of every enemy. It vindicates the faithful and manifests the authority of the first-resurrection company. It restrains Satan's deception and changes the condition of the nations. It advances the divine purpose to the point at which the final rebellion can be exposed and removed, so that no enemy remains when the final state arrives.

Thus the millennium is a kingdom bridge between Christ's visible return and the fully realized new creation. It is part of the ordered wisdom of God, not an unnecessary parenthesis.

The Hope of the Kingdom

The doctrine of the millennial reign is a doctrine of hope. It declares that Christ's return is not merely the end of rebellion but the beginning of open righteous administration. It affirms that the faithful are not forgotten but exalted into service. It shows that Satan's power over the nations is not endless. It confirms that the promises of kingship, priesthood, and kingdom inheritance are real. And it demonstrates that God's purpose for the world moves in ordered stages toward complete restoration.

The millennium also protects the biblical doctrine of the kingdom from reduction. The kingdom is not merely inward experience in the present age. Nor is it only the final eternal state after all history has ended. It includes the thousand-year reign of Christ, in which His victory is openly administered, His faithful ones reign with Him, and His enemies are progressively brought to nothing.

For that reason, the millennial reign must be treated neither with neglect nor with sensationalism. It is not a field for unchecked speculation. It is a revealed part of God's redemptive order. Scripture gives enough to establish its reality, its sequence, its participants, and its purpose. That is enough to shape hope, steady faith, and direct the mind to the triumph of Christ.

The Reign of Christ Before the Final State

The thousand-year reign of Christ stands as a glorious testimony to the orderliness of God's kingdom purpose. Christ returns before it. The blessed and holy who share in the first resurrection reign with Him. Satan is bound so that he can no longer deceive the nations in the same way. The reign is royal, priestly, judicial, and restorative in purpose. It is followed by the final rebellion, the destruction of Satan, the great white throne, and the arrival of the new heaven and new earth.

The millennium therefore cannot be brushed aside as a minor prophetic detail. It is part of the revealed way in which Christ's triumph unfolds in history. The King does not merely appear and instantly move all things into final-state perfection. He appears, destroys the present wicked order, binds the dragon, reigns with His faithful ones, judges mankind in righteousness, and advances the divine purpose in ordered steps until every enemy is abolished.

The millennial reign thus belongs to the Christian hope. It confirms that Christ's victory is not abstract. It is administered. It confirms that the faithful who belong to the first resurrection are not only saved but called to reign with Him. It confirms that the broader kingdom hope moves toward full restoration under the righteous government of God. The thousand years are therefore not an embarrassment to biblical doctrine. They are one of its clearest declarations that Jesus Christ truly rules, truly will return, and truly will bring every enemy under His feet until the whole purpose of Jehovah stands complete.

Chapter 12 — The Final Defeat of Satan

The End of the Ancient Adversary

The final defeat of Satan stands as one of the climactic acts in the biblical revelation of God's kingdom. From the opening chapters of Scripture, where the serpent appears as deceiver and corrupter (Gen. 3:1–5), to the closing visions of Revelation, where the Devil is judged and removed forever (Rev. 20:10), the Bible presents one continuous conflict between the purpose of Jehovah and the rebellion of the evil one. Satan is never portrayed as an equal rival to God. He is creaturely, dependent, limited, and already marked for destruction. Yet he is real, active, malignant, and destructive. He deceives the nations, opposes the holy ones, empowers the beastly order, and wages war against the truth (Job 1:6–12; Zech. 3:1–2; John 8:44; Rev. 12:9, 17; 13:2).

The final defeat of Satan therefore means the final removal of the oldest and deepest personal source of anti-God rebellion in the created order.

This defeat is not an isolated event detached from the rest of biblical prophecy. It belongs to the ordered sequence of Christ's victory. The beast and false prophet are judged at the return of Christ (Rev. 19:20). Satan is then bound for a thousand years so that he should not deceive the nations any longer until the thousand years are completed (Rev. 20:1–3). After that period he is released for a short time, deceives the nations once more, gathers them for final rebellion, and is then cast into the lake of fire (Rev. 20:7–10). The sequence is deliberate. The dragon who stood behind the beastly order is first restrained, then finally destroyed. This ordered judgment demonstrates both divine sovereignty and divine justice. God does not merely crush evil by raw force. He exposes it, restrains it, allows it to reveal itself fully, and then judges it without remainder.

The final defeat of Satan also completes a long biblical expectation. Jehovah told the serpent in Eden that the seed of the woman would bruise his head (Gen. 3:15). That promise reaches its fullest public realization only when Satan is destroyed forever. Christ has already secured the decisive victory through His death and resurrection, disarming the hostile powers and breaking the claim of sin and death (John 12:31; Col. 2:15; Heb. 2:14–15). Yet Revelation shows that the final public abolition of Satan still lies ahead in the outworking of God's kingdom. The cross guarantees the outcome. Revelation displays the final application of that victory.

Satan Bound for a Thousand Years

Revelation 20 begins with a vision of decisive restraint. John says, "And I saw an angel coming down out of heaven, having the key of the abyss and a great chain in his hand. And he seized the dragon, the original serpent, who is the Devil and Satan, and bound him for a thousand years" (Rev. 20:1–2). The text is explicit in identifying the one bound. The dragon is the original serpent of Genesis, the Devil, the slanderer, and Satan, the adversary. The symbolism of the chain and abyss signifies real restraint under divine authority. This is not a vague weakening. It is binding with purpose.

That purpose is stated plainly: Satan is thrown into the abyss, shut in, and sealed over "so that he would not deceive the nations any longer, until the thousand years were completed" (Rev. 20:3). The focus is on his deceiving influence over the nations. During the millennial reign, the dragon is no longer permitted to exercise that same global deceptive power that characterized the age of beastly rebellion. This follows directly after the destruction of the beast and false prophet in Revelation 19. The one who empowered the anti-God political-religious system is now himself restrained. The nations are no longer under the same dragonic seduction that brought them into open war against God and His Christ.

This binding must be read in its own place in the sequence. It does not describe the entire present church age, for Revelation places it after Christ's return in chapter 19 and before Satan's later release in chapter 20. Nor does it describe Satan's final destruction, for Revelation explicitly says he must be released for a short time after the thousand years are completed (Rev. 20:3). The binding therefore marks a real kingdom period in which satanic deception is decisively curtailed while Christ reigns and the faithful of the first resurrection reign with Him (Rev. 20:4–6).

This period also shows that Satan's power is never autonomous. He does not come and go at will. He is seized, bound, imprisoned, released, and destroyed according to divine decree. Revelation therefore strips Satan of every illusion of independence. The dragon who deceived the world is himself subject to the timetable and judgment of God.

The Meaning of Satan's Release

After the thousand years, Revelation states, "Satan will be released from his prison" (Rev. 20:7). This release has often troubled readers, but it serves a profound purpose in the revelation of divine justice. The release does not undo Christ's victory. It does not suggest failure in the kingdom. It does not restore the former beastly regime. Rather, it exposes the enduring reality of rebellion wherever hearts are not steadfastly loyal to God.

John says that Satan will "go out to deceive the nations which are in the four corners of the earth, Gog and Magog, to gather them together for the war" (Rev. 20:8). The names Gog and Magog recall Ezekiel 38–39, where the enemies of God's people gather for a doomed attack under divine judgment. Revelation takes up that imagery to portray the final global rebellion against the kingdom of God. The point is not a narrow ethnic identification but a theological one. The nations once more become the object of satanic deception, and they gather in hostile opposition to God's holy order.

This release reveals that evil cannot be blamed merely on external conditions. During the thousand-year reign, Satan's deceptive influence is restrained, Christ's rule is openly manifested, and the kingdom order advances. Yet when Satan is released, rebellion again surfaces among the nations. This means the final rebellion exposes the moral reality of opposition to God. It demonstrates that evil is not only a matter of bad environment, political disorder, or satanic pressure from without. When given opportunity, those not established in loyalty to God align themselves with deception again. The final release thus vindicates divine justice by showing that rebellion, when judged at the end, is truly deserving of judgment.

This also means that the final defeat of Satan is not arbitrary. God allows the dragon one final release, not because Satan deserves another opportunity, but because the last rebellion must be fully exposed before it is finally destroyed. The universe will see openly that the dragon remains the deceiver to the end, and that those who follow him do so in conscious opposition to the rule of God.

The Final Rebellion Against the Holy Ones

The nations deceived by Satan are described as numerous "like the sand of the sea" (Rev. 20:8). They "came up on the broad plain of the earth and surrounded the camp of the holy ones and the beloved city" (Rev. 20:9). The language is military and covenantal. The final rebellion is not merely inner unbelief. It is organized hostility directed against the people and order of God. Once again, the deepest issue is allegiance. Satan gathers the nations, not for self-defense, but for war against the holy ones.

The "camp of the holy ones" and "the beloved city" should not be handled in crude literalism detached from biblical theology. The imagery points to the covenant people of God under divine favor and protection. The final rebellion is directed against the holy order established under Christ's reign. It is the last attempt of satanic opposition to overthrow or defy the kingdom of God. The nations do not repent under Satan's influence. They assemble for confrontation.

This scene recalls numerous Old Testament patterns in which the nations rage against Jehovah's people and are judged for it (Ps. 2:1–6; Ezek. 38:14–23; Zech. 14:2–3). Yet Revelation intensifies the pattern by placing it at the very end of Satan's career. The dragon who once energized the beast now gathers the nations one final time. The rebellious world, even after all prior judgments, still manifests its hatred of God when deceived by the adversary.

This shows with terrible clarity that apart from divine grace and steadfast loyalty to God, fallen mankind does not move naturally toward submission. Even after the manifest reign of Christ, Satan's release becomes the occasion for exposed rebellion. The final attack thus reveals the depth of anti-God opposition and removes every excuse from the judgment that follows.

Fire From Heaven and the Destruction of the Rebels

The rebellion ends with startling brevity: "and fire came down from heaven and devoured them" (Rev. 20:9). No prolonged battle follows. There is no suspense. The rebellious nations surround the holy ones, and divine judgment falls immediately. The fire from heaven recalls repeated Old Testament scenes in which Jehovah judges His enemies directly and decisively (Gen. 19:24; Lev. 10:2; 2 Kgs. 1:10–12; Ezek. 38:22). Revelation uses that imagery to show that the final rebellion is answered by direct divine destruction.

The verb "devoured" is especially important. It signifies consuming judgment. The rebels are not preserved indefinitely in a living counter-kingdom. They are consumed under divine sentence. This is consistent with the wider biblical language of the destruction of the wicked. Fire in judgment is not merely spectacle. It is the means by which God removes what opposes His holiness. The final rebellion ends, not in negotiation, but in complete defeat.

This scene also highlights the effortless supremacy of God. The nations may be numerous. Satan may deceive them. They may surround the camp of the holy ones. Yet no real threat to divine sovereignty exists. Fire from heaven devours them. The kingdom of God is not shaken. The holy ones are not finally overcome. The last rebellion collapses under the immediate act of God.

Thus Revelation makes clear that the final rebellion is both real and futile. It is real because the nations truly gather against God. It is futile because they can do nothing against Him. Their destruction is swift, total, and judicial. The last uprising of evil in history ends in divine fire.

The Devil Thrown Into the Lake of Fire

After the destruction of the rebellious nations, John records the climactic judgment of Satan himself: "And the Devil who deceived them was thrown into the lake of fire and sulfur, where the beast and the false prophet are also" (Rev. 20:10). This is the final defeat of Satan. The deceiver of the nations, the accuser of the holy ones, the dragon behind the beastly order, the ancient serpent of Eden, is cast into the place of final judgment.

This judgment comes after the beast and false prophet have already been thrown into the lake of fire at Christ's return (Rev. 19:20). Satan's judgment therefore completes the destruction of the entire anti-God order: first the beastly political-religious powers, then the dragon himself. Nothing remains of the rebellious kingdom once this sentence is carried out. The source, the instruments, and the followers of rebellion are all judged in due order.

The significance of this act cannot be overstated. The great enemy of God's people is not merely restrained forever. He is removed from the sphere of history and kingdom life altogether. His influence over the nations ends. His accusations end. His deceptions end. His warfare ends. The one who introduced rebellion into human history is himself finally judged by the King whose victory he could never overturn.

Revelation's language here is severe and solemn. The Devil is cast into the lake of fire, the final realm of divine judgment. In the immediate context of Revelation 20, the lake of fire is later defined as "the second death" when death and Hades and those not found in the book of life are thrown into it (Rev. 20:14–15). This means the final judgment must be understood in harmony with the book's own explanation. The lake of fire is the realm of final, irreversible judgment under God. Satan's destruction is therefore not a temporary defeat or a symbolic humiliation. It is the final removal of the adversary under divine sentence.

The Full Establishment of Divine Justice

The final defeat of Satan brings divine justice into full open establishment. Throughout history, Satan has deceived, accused, tempted, corrupted, and energized the powers of rebellion. He has stood behind false worship, lawless self-exaltation, beastly empire, and persecution of the holy ones. Yet for much of history the moral order of the world has appeared obscured. The wicked prosper. The righteous suffer. The deceiver works in darkness and disguise. The final defeat of Satan ends that obscurity forever.

Divine justice is fully established because every enemy is judged in due order. The beast and false prophet are judged at Christ's return (Rev. 19:20). Satan is bound during the thousand years (Rev. 20:1–3). He is released and allowed to expose rebellion once more (Rev. 20:7–8). The nations who follow him are devoured by fire from heaven (Rev. 20:9). Then Satan himself is cast into the lake of fire (Rev. 20:10). After that comes the great white throne, where the dead are judged and death itself is thrown into the lake of fire (Rev. 20:11–15). The sequence reveals a universe in which no evil is left unaddressed, no rebellion goes unanswered, and no hostile power escapes the judgment of God.

This is why the final defeat of Satan is more than the removal of one enemy. It is the public vindication of the whole moral order of God's kingdom. The dragon who opposed truth is judged. The holy ones are vindicated. The nations learn openly that rebellion against Jehovah ends in destruction. The final state that follows is therefore not built on unresolved evil. It is built on fully executed justice.

This also explains why Revelation can move from Satan's destruction to the new heaven and new earth without contradiction. The old order must be judged before the new order can appear in its fullness. Satan's final removal is one of the last great judicial acts necessary before the final restored creation stands complete.

The End of Satan's Influence Over the Nations

One of the major emphases of Revelation 20 is that Satan's influence over the nations is brought to an end. At the beginning of the chapter he is bound so that he should not deceive the nations any longer during the thousand years (Rev. 20:3). At the end of the chapter he is destroyed after his final deceptive work is exposed and judged (Rev. 20:10). Thus the whole chapter frames the end of satanic deception over the nations.

This is important because the nations have long been the sphere of dragonic delusion in biblical prophecy. The beast receives authority over every tribe and people and tongue and nation (Rev. 13:7). The false prophet deceives those who dwell on the earth by signs (Rev. 13:14). The kings of the earth are gathered for rebellion under the influence of unclean spirits like frogs coming from the dragon, the beast, and the false prophet (Rev. 16:13–16). Babylon intoxicates the nations with her immorality and idolatry (Rev. 17:2; 18:3). The end of Satan's influence therefore means the end of the entire global pattern of deception that dominated the age of rebellion.

When Satan is finally destroyed, the nations are no longer subject to his seduction. The source of anti-God deceit is gone. The adversary who moved rulers, systems, false religion, and rebellious peoples against God is removed from the created order. This is one of the great blessings secured by the victory of Christ. The nations no longer live under the shadow of dragonic manipulation. The whole structure of deceit is ended.

The Final Defeat of Satan and the Hope of the Holy Ones

For the holy ones, the final defeat of Satan is not abstract doctrine. It is covenant comfort. Throughout Scripture Satan appears as adversary of God's people. He accuses Joshua the high priest (Zech. 3:1). He seeks to sift the disciples (Luke 22:31). He blinds the minds of unbelievers (2 Cor. 4:4). He prowls like a roaring lion seeking someone to devour (1 Pet. 5:8). He wages war against those who keep the commandments of God and hold to the testimony of Jesus (Rev. 12:17). The final destruction of Satan therefore means the end of that warfare forever.

No more accusation will rise against the holy ones. No more deception will threaten the nations. No more beastly empire will be energized by the dragon. No more false prophet will sacralize rebellion. No more mark of the beast will divide humanity by allegiance to a counterfeit kingdom. The enemy behind all these things will be gone.

This means the final defeat of Satan is one of the greatest assurances that the kingdom of God is permanent, pure, and secure. The new creation that follows is not fragile. It is not threatened by another future uprising of evil. The dragon is destroyed. The adversary is gone. The old deceiver will never again enter the story of God's people. Divine justice has fully answered him.

The Moral Meaning of History

The final defeat of Satan also reveals the moral meaning of history. Evil has not been ultimate. Deception has not gone unanswered. The apparent successes of the dragon have always been temporary. Revelation 20 shows that the history of rebellion moves toward judgment, not triumph. Satan may deceive, gather, accuse, and war, but he cannot overturn the decree of God. His very release after the thousand years serves God's purpose of exposing evil fully before its final destruction.

Thus history is not the story of two equal powers locked in endless struggle. It is the story of Jehovah's sovereign purpose moving through conflict toward complete victory in Christ. The dragon enters the story as deceiver. He exits the story as condemned enemy. The holy ones endure in the middle, but they endure with certainty because the end has been revealed.

This moral meaning gives the church strength. The people of God need not fear that evil is timeless, invincible, or woven permanently into the structure of reality. Satan's defeat means evil has an end. The nations will not always be deceived. The saints will not always suffer. The dragon will not always accuse. There is a final defeat, and that defeat belongs to the revealed purpose of God.

The End of the Adversary

The final defeat of Satan is one of the brightest vindications of the kingdom of God. The dragon is bound, released, exposed, and destroyed. His influence over the nations is brought to an end. His final rebellion is crushed by fire from heaven. Divine justice is fully established. The adversary who stood behind the serpent's lie, the beast's power, the false prophet's deception, and the nations' rage is removed from the created order forever.

This defeat is not partial. It is not symbolic in a way that empties it of finality. It is the ultimate destruction of Satan under the righteous judgment of God. The one who deceived the nations is himself judged. The one who opposed the holy ones is forever removed from their future. The one who stood behind the anti-God order is cast into the realm of final judgment. After this, the way is clear for the great white throne, the abolition of death, and the new heaven and new earth.

The church therefore looks forward not only to the return of Christ, the resurrection of the dead, and the judgment of the wicked, but also to the complete end of Satan himself. The final defeat of the Devil means the final safety of God's people, the final cleansing of the nations, and the final vindication of Jehovah's righteous rule. The ancient serpent will deceive no more. The dragon will rage no more. The adversary will accuse no more. The kingdom of God will stand without rival, without corruption, and without end.

Chapter 13 — The New Heaven and New Earth

The Final Goal of God's Kingdom Purpose

Biblical prophecy does not end with judgment alone. It ends with restoration. The destruction of the beastly order, the defeat of Satan, the resurrection of the dead, and the judgment of the wicked all serve a larger purpose in the will of God. They clear the way for the final renewal of creation under His righteous rule. Scripture directs the hope of the faithful, not toward an endless abstraction, nor toward a merely spiritual existence detached from the created order, but toward a new heaven and a new earth in which righteousness dwells (Isa. 65:17; 66:22; 2 Pet. 3:13; Rev. 21:1).

This is one of the most neglected and misunderstood themes in Christian doctrine. Many have assumed that the ultimate hope of the righteous is simply to leave the earth forever and dwell in heaven in an unembodied or purely celestial condition. But the Bible presents a different and fuller picture. A select company is indeed granted the heavenly calling and reigns with Christ (Luke 12:32; Rev. 5:9–10; 20:4–6). Yet the broader biblical hope includes the restoration of the earth as the sphere of everlasting life under God's kingdom. The final vision of Scripture is not souls escaping creation, but creation itself renewed, cleansed, and brought into harmony with the purpose of Jehovah.

This is why Revelation 21–22 and Isaiah 65–66 are so important. They do not merely provide decorative imagery for religious comfort. They reveal the consummation of God's purpose for man, the earth, and the kingdom. What was lost through sin is not abandoned. It is restored under the triumph of Christ. The curse is removed. Death is gone. Tears are wiped away. The dwelling of God is with men. The river of life flows. The tree of life yields its fruit. The nations are healed. The righteous live forever under the light of God and the Lamb (Rev. 21:3–4, 23–27; 22:1–5).

Thus the new heaven and new earth are not an appendix to prophecy. They are its goal. Judgment is severe because restoration is glorious. Evil is removed because everlasting righteousness is God's purpose. The final hope of Scripture is therefore not merely the end of suffering, but the beginning of a renewed creation fully ordered under Jehovah's kingdom.

"A New Heaven and a New Earth"

Revelation 21 opens with one of the most sweeping declarations in all Scripture: "And I saw a new heaven and a new earth; for the first heaven and the first earth passed away, and the sea is no more" (Rev. 21:1). The language immediately recalls Isaiah 65:17, where Jehovah says, "For look! I am creating new heavens and a new earth; and the former things will not be called to mind, neither will they come up into the heart." Isaiah 66:22 repeats the same promise, linking the endurance of the new heavens and new earth with the enduring name and offspring of God's people. Peter also says, "according to His promise we are looking for new heavens and a new earth, in which righteousness dwells" (2 Pet. 3:13). The consistency of this language across both Testaments shows that the hope is deeply rooted and not confined to one apocalyptic passage.

The expression "new heaven and new earth" must be interpreted with biblical care. It does not require the annihilation of all created substance followed by the creation of an utterly unrelated universe. The biblical emphasis is on renewal, replacement of the old order of sin and death, and the arrival of a new order governed by righteousness. The present heavens and earth in their fallen, curse-marked, rebellious condition pass away as the dominant order. What comes is new in quality, righteousness, condition, and relation to God.

This is already suggested by Isaiah's usage. Isaiah 65 does not describe an abstract nonmaterial world detached from earthly life. It describes joy, building, planting, peace, and the end of former sorrow under God's renewed order (Isa. 65:18–25). The newness therefore does not point away from creation, but toward creation restored to its intended harmony. Likewise, Peter contrasts the present order marked by ungodliness with the coming order in which righteousness dwells (2 Pet. 3:7, 13). The primary contrast is moral and covenantal. The old rebellious system gives way to the new righteous one.

Revelation's language also indicates this. The first heaven and first earth pass away because the old order of death, mourning, crying, pain, curse, rebellion, and separation from God must be removed. The "sea" being no more is part of that same symbolic transformation. In Revelation the sea is repeatedly associated with restlessness, danger, and the sphere out of which beastly power arises (Rev. 13:1; compare Dan. 7:2–3). The point is not that the new creation must be imagined as a geographical statement only, but that the old order of chaos and hostility to God is gone.

Thus the new heaven and new earth signify the final renewal of creation under the full triumph of God's kingdom. The old order passes. The righteous order remains.

The Holy City Comes Down

One of the most decisive features of Revelation 21 is the movement of the holy city. John says, "And I saw the holy city, New Jerusalem, coming down out of heaven from God, prepared as a bride adorned for her husband" (Rev. 21:2). This movement is theological and immensely important. The city does not rise up from earth into heaven. It comes down out of heaven to earth. The direction of the image shows that God's purpose is not to abandon the earth, but to bring heavenly rule, holiness, and blessing to it.

New Jerusalem is both city and bride. It is ordered life under God's rule, and it is the people in covenant beauty and purity before Him. The imagery is rich, but its meaning is plain. The final order of redemption is not a disembodied abstraction. It is the descent of God's holy arrangement into the realm where redeemed humanity lives. Heaven's government comes down. God's holy city comes down. The result is not escape from created life, but created life brought into full harmony with heaven.

This is exactly what Jesus taught His disciples to pray: "Let Your kingdom come. Let Your will take place, as in heaven, also upon earth" (Matt. 6:10). Revelation 21 is the final answer to that prayer. The heavenly order is no longer opposed by the earthly realm. The will of God is done without resistance. The holy city comes down, and the dwelling of God is with men.

This also helps clarify the role of the heavenly calling in relation to the earth. The select company associated with the New Jerusalem is not removed from the final picture of restored earthly life. Rather, the heavenly city itself descends in relation to the earth. Those who reign with Christ belong to the heavenly administration of the kingdom, but the outworking of that reign blesses the restored creation. The final vision is therefore not purely heavenly in the sense of excluding the earth. It is heavenly rule brought into perfect relation with earthly restoration.

"The Tent of God Is With Men"

After seeing the holy city, John hears a loud voice from the throne saying, "Look! The tent of God is with men, and He will dwell with them, and they will be His peoples, and God Himself will be with them" (Rev. 21:3). No statement could more directly reveal the final goal of redemption. God dwells with men. The issue is not merely that men go to dwell with God elsewhere. The emphasis is that God's presence is with redeemed mankind in the new order.

This language draws on the whole history of divine dwelling. Jehovah dwelt symbolically with Israel in the tabernacle and temple (Exod. 25:8; 1 Kgs. 8:10–13). He promised through the prophets that He would dwell in the midst of His people in the restored order (Ezek. 37:26–28; Zech. 2:10–11). Revelation brings that promise to final realization. There is no more mediated distance in the old sense. God's dwelling is with men in permanent covenant nearness.

This should shape the doctrine of eternal life profoundly. The final hope is not defined merely by location. It is defined by the restored presence of God. Wherever God dwells with His redeemed in unhindered favor, that is blessedness. Revelation 21 declares that this blessing belongs to men in the new creation. The restored order is not godless earthiness. It is earth renewed under the direct favor and presence of God.

This also means that the biblical hope of eternal life on earth is not inferior or secondary in a dismissive sense. It is life where God dwells with men. It is covenant fullness. It is fellowship under His light, His peace, and His kingdom. The earth was always meant to be the sphere of man's blessed life under God (Gen. 1:26–28; Ps. 115:16). Sin disrupted that purpose. Redemption restores it.

No More Death, Mourning, Crying, or Pain

The next words in Revelation 21 are among the most beloved in all Scripture: "And He will wipe away every tear from their eyes; and death will be no more, neither will mourning nor outcry nor pain be anymore. The former things have passed away" (Rev. 21:4). These words gather into one promise the whole reversal of the curse. Death, grief, anguish, and suffering belong to the old order. They entered the human story through sin and have marked all of man's history under alienation from God (Gen. 3:16–19; Rom. 5:12). But they do not belong to the final state of redeemed creation. In the new heaven and new earth, they are gone because the conditions that produced them are gone.

The statement that "death will be no more" is especially decisive. Death is not treated here as a necessary feature of creaturely existence, nor as an eternal companion to life. It is an enemy, and in the final order that enemy has been abolished (1 Cor. 15:26). Revelation has already shown death and Hades being thrown into the lake of fire, which is the second death (Rev. 20:14). The new creation therefore stands on the far side of death's destruction. Eternal life is no longer lived under the shadow of mortality. The curse has been removed from the human condition.

The wiping away of tears is equally tender and profound. God does not merely end the causes of sorrow in an abstract sense. He personally removes the tears of His people. This is covenant intimacy in its fullest expression. The God who once seemed distant in a world of pain now dwells with His people and removes the marks of grief from their faces. Isaiah had already spoken in similar language: Jehovah "will swallow up death forever, and the Lord Jehovah will wipe tears from all faces" (Isa. 25:8). Revelation shows that ancient promise fulfilled in the final restoration.

This means the new earth is not merely a repaired environment. It is a healed order of life in which the deepest wounds of history are answered. Mourning ends because death ends. Pain ends because the curse ends. Outcry ceases because oppression, injustice, and loss no longer define the human condition. The final hope of Scripture is therefore not escape from embodiment, but the restoration of embodied life under conditions where sorrow has no place.

"I Am Making All Things New"

The promise of restoration is then reinforced by the voice from the throne: "Look! I am making all things new" (Rev. 21:5). This declaration comes from the One seated on the throne, the sovereign God whose purpose cannot fail. The language is active and comprehensive. He is making all things new. The emphasis falls not on the destruction of creation as though matter itself were evil, but on the renewal of all things under divine power.

This harmonizes with the wider biblical witness. Peter spoke of "times of restoration of all things" foretold by the prophets (Acts 3:21). Paul wrote that creation itself will be set free from slavery to corruption into the freedom of the glory of the children of God (Rom. 8:19–21). Isaiah described a new heavens and new earth in which former troubles are forgotten and rejoicing replaces grief (Isa. 65:17–19). Revelation gathers these themes and gives them final expression. The God who created the world good in the beginning does not abandon His purpose for it. He renews it.

The same voice then says, "These words are faithful and true" (Rev. 21:5). That assurance matters because the promise is so sweeping that faith might waver before it. But the final restoration does not depend on human optimism. It depends on the faithfulness of God. He is the Alpha and the Omega, the beginning and the end (Rev. 21:6). What He began in creation and covenant, He will complete in redemption and renewal.

This also guards the doctrine of restoration from sentimentality. The new creation is not wishful thinking. It is the decreed outcome of God's kingdom purpose. The One who promises it is the One who judged Babylon, destroyed the beast, bound Satan, raised the dead, and abolished the old order. The same power that executes judgment establishes the new creation. Thus restoration is not fragile hope. It is certain hope.

The Inheritance of the Faithful

Revelation 21 then makes the promise personal: "The one who conquers will inherit these things, and I will be his God and he will be My son" (Rev. 21:7). The final restoration is not indiscriminate universalism. It is covenant inheritance. The one who conquers inherits. Throughout Revelation, conquering means remaining faithful to God and to the testimony of Jesus in the face of pressure, deception, suffering, and beastly opposition (Rev. 2:7, 11, 17, 26; 3:5, 12, 21; 12:11). The new creation belongs to those who endured in loyalty.

That inheritance language reaches back into the whole biblical story. Abraham looked for the fulfillment of divine promise (Gen. 12:1–3; Heb. 11:8–10). The meek were promised that they would inherit the earth (Ps. 37:11; Matt. 5:5). Daniel's holy ones were told they would receive the kingdom (Dan. 7:18, 27). Revelation now shows the consummation of that inheritance. The faithful inherit restored creation, covenant nearness, and everlasting life under God's rule.

The filial language is equally significant: "I will be his God and he will be My son." This does not erase the distinction between Christ as the unique Son and believers as adopted sons. Rather, it expresses the fullness of redeemed covenant relationship. The final state is not merely legal acquittal or environmental blessing. It is familial nearness to God. The faithful do not merely survive into eternity. They belong to God in a perfected covenant bond.

The Exclusion of the Wicked

Immediately after this promise, Revelation states the opposite outcome: "But as for the cowardly and unbelieving and those who are abominable and murderers and sexually immoral persons and sorcerers and idolaters and all the liars, their part will be in the lake that burns with fire and sulfur, which is the second death" (Rev. 21:8). The new creation is therefore not morally mixed. It is not a restored world in which evil continues alongside righteousness. The wicked are excluded because the second death has removed them from the final order.

This verse is important because it shows that the new heaven and new earth stand only after final judgment has done its work. The holy city is holy because what is unclean has been removed. Eternal life on the renewed earth is secure because the rebellious are no longer present to corrupt it. The biblical hope is not that good and evil coexist forever in unresolved tension. It is that evil is finally judged and righteousness dwells without rival.

The phrase "second death" again confirms the nature of final punishment. The wicked do not inherit eternal life in another form. They are consigned to the second death. This makes the blessedness of the new creation all the more profound. There is no lurking counter-kingdom, no immortal realm of evil parallel to the kingdom of God. The restored order is genuinely cleansed.

The Glory of New Jerusalem

John then returns to the holy city in greater detail. One of the angels carries him away and shows him "the holy city Jerusalem coming down out of heaven from God, having the glory of God" (Rev. 21:10–11). The city shines with divine splendor. Its brilliance is likened to a very costly stone, like crystal-clear jasper. The imagery is radiant because the city reflects the holiness and glory of God Himself.

The city's great and high wall, its twelve gates, and its twelve foundation stones symbolize security, access, and covenant completeness (Rev. 21:12–14). The gates bear the names of the twelve tribes of the sons of Israel, while the foundations bear the names of the twelve apostles of the Lamb. The imagery unites the people of God across the whole history of redemption. The city is not a private possession of one age only. It is the perfected covenant community in its complete fullness under God and the Lamb.

Its measured perfection, its cube-like dimensions, and its use of precious materials all communicate holiness, fullness, and divine design (Rev. 21:15–21). The city is not chaotic. It is ordered. It is not defiled. It is pure. It is not insecure. It is established forever. The symbolism is architectural, but the meaning is theological. God's redeemed order is complete, beautiful, secure, and holy.

The city also has no temple in it, "for the Lord God the Almighty and the Lamb are its temple" (Rev. 21:22). This does not diminish worship. It fulfills it. In the former order, temple structures mediated divine presence. In the final order, God and the Lamb are directly present. No separate sanctuary is needed because the whole city exists in unhindered relation to God. This is one of the clearest signs that the final restoration is the realization of all covenant hopes.

The Nations in the Light of God

Revelation then says the city has no need of sun or moon to shine upon it, "for the glory of God illumined it, and its lamp is the Lamb" (Rev. 21:23). The imagery does not deny that God created the heavenly lights good, but it emphasizes that the final source of life, order, and blessedness is the direct glory of God mediated through the Lamb. Darkness, symbolic and actual, has no rule there. The Lamb who was slain now shines as the lamp of the holy city.

John adds that "the nations will walk by its light, and the kings of the earth bring their glory into it" (Rev. 21:24). This is a crucial statement for the doctrine of restored life on earth. The language of nations shows that the final vision is not a purely heavenly abstraction cut off from the life of mankind on a renewed earth. The nations live in relation to the city's light. They are not in rebellion, not intoxicated by Babylon, and not deceived by the dragon. They walk by the light of God and the Lamb.

This fits the wider prophetic pattern. Isaiah had said, "nations will come to your light, and kings to the brightness of your rising" (Isa. 60:3). Revelation takes up that promise and places it in the final order. The nations are not annihilated as a human category; they are healed, ordered, and illuminated under the kingdom of God. The kings bring their glory into the city, not as rival sovereigns, but as those whose honor is subordinated to the supreme glory of God.

The gates of the city are never shut by day, "for there will be no night there" (Rev. 21:25). Open gates signify security, peace, and free access in righteousness. There is nothing threatening outside, no need for defensive closure, no lurking enemy in the darkness. The old city of man needed walls against danger. The holy city has walls, but its gates remain open because peace is complete.

Nothing unclean will ever enter it, nor anyone practicing abomination and lying, "but only those who are written in the Lamb's book of life" (Rev. 21:27). Holiness remains the defining feature of the restored order. The nations walk by its light, but the city is not morally diluted by their presence. Everything in the final creation exists under the purity of God's kingdom.

The River of the Water of Life

Revelation 22 continues the vision by showing "a river of water of life, bright as crystal, proceeding out of the throne of God and of the Lamb" (Rev. 22:1). This river is one of the most powerful images of life in all Scripture. It recalls Eden, where a river watered the garden (Gen. 2:10), and Ezekiel 47, where a life-giving river flows from the temple and brings healing wherever it goes. Revelation gathers those themes and places them in the final order. Life flows from the throne itself. The source of life is God and the Lamb.

This river is not merely scenic imagery. It represents the unending outflow of divine life, blessing, and provision in the restored creation. The life given to the righteous is not autonomous self-existence. It continues in dependent relation to God, who is the fountain of life (Ps. 36:9). Eternal life on the renewed earth is therefore not independent immortality in the absolute sense. It is life sustained by God's kingdom provision, flowing from His throne.

This accords perfectly with the broader biblical distinction between immortality and eternal life. The heavenly co-rulers who share in the first resurrection are associated with immortality in the strict Pauline sense. The broader righteous, however, are repeatedly described as inheriting everlasting life under God's restored order. The imagery of the river of life fits that broader hope beautifully. Life on the renewed earth is everlasting because it flows from God and the Lamb without interruption or curse.

The Tree of Life and the Healing of the Nations

John also sees "on this side of the river and on that was the tree of life, producing twelve crops of fruit, yielding its fruit every month; and the leaves of the tree were for the healing of the nations" (Rev. 22:2). The tree of life first appears in Eden, where access to it was barred after man's sin so that fallen man would not live forever in that cursed condition (Gen. 2:9; 3:22–24). Revelation closes the biblical story by restoring access to the tree of life in the new creation. What was lost at the fall is restored through redemption.

The continual fruitfulness of the tree shows abundance, stability, and unending provision. The healing of the nations does not imply the presence of disease in the final state as though the nations remained partly fallen. Rather, it signifies the full restorative blessing that now belongs to them under God's kingdom. The nations once deceived, wounded, and corrupted are now the recipients of the life and health of the new creation.

This is one of the strongest images in all Scripture for eternal life on earth under God's kingdom. The nations are there. The tree of life is there. Healing is there. Access to life is there. The curse that once cut man off from Eden is gone. Revelation is not pointing away from creation but toward its final blessedness.

No More Curse

John then states it plainly: "There will no longer be any curse" (Rev. 22:3). This brief statement gathers up the whole tragedy of Genesis 3 and announces its final reversal. The ground was cursed because of sin (Gen. 3:17). Pain, toil, frustration, and death entered human existence. Creation was subjected to futility (Rom. 8:20). But in the final order, the curse is no more. Everything associated with alienation from God has been removed.

Instead of the curse, "the throne of God and of the Lamb will be in it, and His slaves will serve Him" (Rev. 22:3). Service is no longer burden under futility. It is joyful worship in the direct presence of God. "They will see His face, and His name will be on their foreheads" (Rev. 22:4). To see God's face is the language of unhindered favor, covenant intimacy, and full acceptance. His name on their foreheads signifies belonging, identity, and open loyalty. The mark of the beast is forever gone. Only the name of God remains upon His people.

"There will no longer be any night," John says, "and they will not have need of the light of a lamp nor the light of the sun, because the Lord God will illumine them; and they will reign forever and ever" (Rev. 22:5). The reign language here belongs most directly to those associated with the holy city and the heavenly administration of the kingdom. Yet the whole restored order lives under the light and blessing of God's presence. Darkness is gone. The old age has ended. Life now exists entirely under divine illumination.

Isaiah 65 and the Joy of Restored Earthly Life

Isaiah 65 provides a complementary picture of this restored order. Jehovah says, "For look! I am creating new heavens and a new earth" (Isa. 65:17). He then describes Jerusalem as a cause for rejoicing and her people as a joy (Isa. 65:18–19). No longer is there weeping and distress. Life is marked by peace, stability, and blessing under divine favor.

The chapter speaks of building houses and inhabiting them, planting vineyards and eating their fruit (Isa. 65:21). This is not the language of a purely heavenly abstraction. It is the language of renewed earthly life. The labor of the righteous is not stolen from them. They do not build for another to inhabit or plant for another to consume. The curse of futility is gone. Their days are "like the days of a tree," and they enjoy the work of their hands (Isa. 65:22).

Isaiah also describes harmony in creation: "The wolf and the lamb will feed together, and the lion will eat straw like the bull" (Isa. 65:25). However one handles the imagery in all its details, the theological point is unmistakable. The new creation is a realm of peace, not violence; harmony, not predation; blessing, not destruction. The prophet is not directing hope away from the earth. He is directing hope toward an earth renewed under God's kingdom.

This is why Isaiah 65 is indispensable to a biblical doctrine of final restoration. It guards against a reduction of the final hope to heaven alone. The prophets looked for renewed earthly life under divine rule. Revelation does not cancel that hope. It brings it to consummation.

The Final Hope Is Not Purely Heavenly Existence

At this point the biblical emphasis must be stated plainly. The final hope of Scripture is not a purely heavenly existence for all the redeemed. A select company is indeed called to heavenly rule with Christ and participates in the first resurrection, priestly service, and kingly reign (Luke 22:28–30; Rev. 5:9–10; 20:4–6). But the broader hope revealed in prophecy is everlasting life on a renewed earth under God's kingdom.

This is why the language of inheriting the earth remains so important. "The meek will possess the earth" (Ps. 37:11; compare Matt. 5:5). "The righteous themselves will possess the earth, and they will reside forever upon it" (Ps. 37:29). These are not marginal texts to be ignored in favor of later assumptions. They belong to the consistent biblical vision of restored life under divine rule.

The descent of New Jerusalem, the dwelling of God with men, the healing of the nations, the removal of the curse, and the promise of everlasting life all point toward that same conclusion. The new heaven and new earth are not the abolition of earthly hope, but its fulfillment. The earth is not discarded as though God's original purpose for man on the earth had failed permanently. It is renewed. The kingdom brings heaven's order to earth, and the righteous live forever under that order.

This does not diminish the heavenly calling. It places it in its proper relation to the wider kingdom purpose. Heaven and earth are not set in final opposition. The heavenly city comes down. The heavenly administration blesses the renewed creation. God dwells with men. The final order is therefore one of harmony, not fragmentation.

Edward D. Andrews

The Everlasting Life of the Righteous

The final chapters of Revelation thus present everlasting life in its fullest biblical form. The righteous have access to the river of life and the tree of life. They live in the presence of God and the Lamb. They are free from death, pain, mourning, and curse. They walk in the light of God's glory. They belong to Him openly and permanently. This is not a temporary millennial arrangement only. It is the everlasting state of redeemed creation.

Here the distinction between immortality and eternal life remains important. The reigning company of the first resurrection receives immortality in relation to heavenly kingship with Christ. The broader righteous inherit everlasting life on the renewed earth. Both are glorious gifts of God, but Scripture does not flatten them into one indistinguishable destiny. Eternal life on earth is not a lesser consolation prize. It is the outworking of God's original and restored purpose for humanity under His kingdom.

John 3:16 speaks with enduring simplicity: those who believe in the Son "will not be destroyed but have eternal life." Matthew 25:46 says the righteous go away into eternal life. Daniel 12:2 speaks of resurrection to everlasting life. Revelation 22 shows that life in its full restored sense. The righteous live forever because God gives them life, sustains them by His throne, and removes forever what would threaten that life.

The Completion of God's Purpose

The new heaven and new earth are therefore the completion of God's kingdom purpose. Creation began with man on earth under God's blessing. Sin brought curse, death, alienation, and expulsion from the tree of life.

Redemption in Christ moves history toward the full reversal of that tragedy. Satan is destroyed. The wicked are judged. Death is abolished. The curse is removed. Access to life is restored. God dwells with men. The nations are healed. Righteousness remains.

This is the end toward which all prophecy moves. The final restoration of creation is not decorative imagery or spiritual metaphor. It is the consummation of what Jehovah purposed from the beginning and secured through the triumph of His Son. The last chapters of Scripture therefore do not leave the reader in uncertainty. They leave him in hope—hope of renewed creation, hope of everlasting life, hope of God's presence, hope of a world where righteousness dwells and evil will never rise again.

The biblical hope is thus neither an endless abstraction nor a merely heavenly relocation of all the redeemed. It is the restoration of all things under the kingdom of God. The holy city comes down. The tent of God is with men. The river of life flows. The tree of life bears fruit. The nations walk in the light. The righteous live forever. The new heaven and new earth stand as the final and glorious answer to the fall, the final and glorious vindication of the kingdom, and the final and glorious home of everlasting righteousness under Jehovah and the Lamb.

Chapter 14 — Living in Readiness for Christ's Return

The Pastoral Force of the Doctrine

The doctrine of the Second Coming is never given in Scripture merely to satisfy curiosity about the future. It is given to shape the life of the faithful in the present. Jesus did not teach His return so that His followers would become obsessed with timetables, restless with speculation, or paralyzed by fear. He taught it so that they would remain watchful, holy, faithful, and steady in doing the will of His Father. The apostles followed the same pattern. They did not present the coming of Christ as material for endless argument. They presented it as a motive for righteous living, steadfast endurance, love of truth, and patient labor in the service of God.

This pastoral emphasis appears throughout the New Testament. Jesus says, "Keep on the watch, because you do not know which day your Lord is coming" (Matt. 24:42). Paul writes, "let us not sleep as the rest do, but let us stay awake and keep our senses" (1 Thess. 5:6). Peter says that "the end of all things has drawn close," and therefore believers must be "sound in mind and self-controlled with a view to prayers" (1 Pet. 4:7). John says, "everyone who has this hope fixed on Him purifies himself just as that one is pure" (1 John 3:3). These texts show the true purpose of prophetic hope. The certainty of Christ's return calls for preparedness rather than speculation, obedience rather than excitement, and perseverance rather than panic.

The church therefore must never treat the return of Christ as a remote doctrine disconnected from ordinary Christian life. It belongs in the center of discipleship. The believer who truly expects the coming of the Lord will not live carelessly. He will not give himself over to spiritual laziness, moral compromise, or worldly self-importance. At the same time, he will not abandon the responsibilities of daily life as though watchfulness meant disorder or neglect. Biblical readiness is neither fanaticism nor indifference. It is ordered, faithful, enduring obedience.

Watchfulness Without Date-Setting

One of the clearest practical lessons drawn from the doctrine of Christ's return is the necessity of watchfulness. Jesus repeatedly emphasized that His followers do not know the day or hour of His coming (Matt. 24:36, 42, 44; 25:13; Mark 13:32–37). That ignorance is not a defect in revelation. It is part of the Lord's design for the moral formation of His people. They are not meant to calculate the date of His return and then arrange obedience around it. They are meant to live in such a way that His return finds them faithful whenever it occurs.

This is why Jesus warns so strongly against false confidence and false claims. "If that evil slave says in his heart, 'My master is delaying,'" and begins to live in violence and indulgence, judgment falls upon him unexpectedly (Matt. 24:48–51). The problem is not merely doctrinal confusion. It is moral carelessness produced by a false sense of delay. In the same way, the foolish virgins of Matthew 25 were unprepared, not because they lacked information about the bridegroom's identity, but because they were not ready when he arrived (Matt. 25:1–13). Readiness is therefore not a matter of prophetic cleverness. It is a matter of sustained faithfulness.

The refusal of date-setting follows directly from this teaching. Jesus said plainly, "concerning that day and hour nobody knows" (Matt. 24:36). Before His ascension He said, "It does not belong to you to know times or seasons which the Father has placed in His own authority" (Acts 1:7). Every attempt to produce certainty where Christ withheld it is therefore an act of presumption. Scripture does not authorize such speculation. It calls for vigilance, not arithmetic. The church dishonors the doctrine of the Second Coming whenever it turns it into a repeated cycle of predictions, disappointments, and sensational alarms.

Watchfulness means something much deeper. It means maintaining righteous standing with God. It means living in repentance, faith, obedience, and truth. It means staying awake morally and spiritually while the world drifts in false peace. It means ordering life so that the coming of Christ would not expose hypocrisy, unrepented sin, or divided allegiance. The Christian who watches is the one who remains loyal.

Holiness as the Proper Response to the Coming King

The expectation of Christ's return is always linked in Scripture to holiness. John says, "Beloved, now we are children of God, and it has not yet been made manifest what we will be. We know that whenever He is made manifest, we will be like Him, because we will see Him just as He is. And everyone who has this hope fixed on Him purifies himself just as that one is pure" (1 John 3:2–3). The logic is direct. Future conformity to Christ requires present purification. The hope of seeing Him produces a life that seeks to please Him now.

Peter speaks in the same way. After describing the coming day of God and the passing away of the present order, he asks, "since all these things are to be dissolved in this way, what sort of people ought you to be in holy conduct and godliness" (2 Pet. 3:11). He then urges believers to be diligent to be found by Christ "spotless and unblemished, and at peace" (2 Pet. 3:14). Prophetic hope therefore does not produce moral looseness. It produces seriousness, self-examination, and the pursuit of holiness.

This holiness must be understood biblically. It is not self-righteous performance or external severity detached from the heart. It is covenant loyalty expressed in obedience to God's Word. It involves rejecting sexual immorality, falsehood, greed, idolatry, bitterness, drunkenness, and every form of lawlessness (1 Cor. 6:9–11; Gal. 5:19–21; Eph. 4:25–32; 5:3–11). It involves walking in the light, confessing sin, loving the brothers, speaking truth, and pursuing what pleases the Lord (1 John 1:7–9; 2:28–29; Eph. 5:8–10).

Edward D. Andrews

The doctrine of Christ's return presses this holiness upon the conscience because it reminds the believer that life is lived before the face of the coming Judge. Secret sin is not truly secret. Hidden corruption will not remain hidden forever. The returning King will expose all falsehood. For that reason, those who wait for Him must put away what belongs to darkness. Readiness is moral before it is chronological.

Faithfulness in the Work God Has Given

Jesus' teaching about readiness is inseparable from faithfulness in assigned work. In the parable of the faithful and evil slave, the faithful servant is the one whom the master finds "doing so" when he comes (Matt. 24:46). In the parable of the talents, the good servants are those who used what was entrusted to them faithfully over time, while the wicked servant buried his talent in fear and negligence (Matt. 25:14–30). In Luke's parallel kingdom parable, the nobleman says, "Do business until I come" (Luke 19:13). These passages show that waiting for Christ is active, not passive. The church is not called to stare at the sky. It is called to be found faithful in the labor assigned by the Master.

This applies to every sphere of obedience. The preacher must preach faithfully. The shepherd must care for the flock faithfully. The husband must love and lead faithfully. The wife must honor God faithfully. Children must obey faithfully. Workers must labor honestly "as to Jehovah and not to men" (Col. 3:23). Those with material resources must use them responsibly. Those with spiritual gifts must exercise them in service. Those entrusted with truth must hold fast to it. Those given opportunities to do good must not neglect them. Readiness is not escape from stewardship. It is intensified stewardship because the Master may return at any time.

Paul closes his great resurrection chapter with precisely this point: "Therefore, my beloved brothers, be steadfast, immovable, always abounding in the work of Jehovah, knowing that your labor is not in vain in Jehovah" (1 Cor. 15:58). The certainty of resurrection and the certainty of Christ's triumph do not lessen daily obedience. They establish it. Labor done in loyalty to God is not wasted. The coming kingdom gives present work its enduring significance.

This protects the doctrine of Christ's return from becoming a theology of passivity. The church is not meant to withdraw from obedience under the excuse of waiting. It is meant to persist in obedience because the coming of Christ gives every act of faithfulness eternal meaning.

Evangelism in the Light of the Coming Judgment

The expectation of Christ's return also sharpens the church's commitment to evangelism. Jesus said, "this gospel of the kingdom will be preached in the whole inhabited earth for a witness to all the nations, and then the end will come" (Matt. 24:14). The church therefore lives between the ascension and the return of Christ as a witnessing people. It announces the kingdom because the King is coming. It calls men to repentance because Judgment Day is fixed. It proclaims salvation because apart from Christ men perish.

This evangelistic urgency appears throughout the apostolic writings. Paul says that God "is now declaring to men that all people everywhere should repent, because He has fixed a day in which He is going to judge the inhabited earth in righteousness" (Acts 17:30–31). Peter says that the seeming delay of the day of the Lord is an expression of God's patience, "not desiring any to be destroyed but all to attain to repentance" (2 Pet. 3:9). The church's task in the present age is therefore not to speculate about hidden matters, but to proclaim the open gospel while the day of mercy remains.

This does not mean the church preaches out of nervous excitement. It preaches out of sober love, urgency, and loyalty to Christ. The same Lord who will come in judgment now commands the gospel to be proclaimed. Those who truly believe He is returning will not be indifferent to the spiritual condition of others. They will desire that men turn from the lie to the truth, from idolatry to the living God, and from the broad road of destruction to the narrow way that leads to life.

Evangelism also guards the doctrine of the Second Coming from selfishness. The return of Christ is not merely the private hope of the believer. It is the public turning point of history. Therefore the church cannot hold the doctrine as a private comfort while neglecting its obligation to bear witness to the world. The people who most earnestly await the coming King should be the people most earnest in proclaiming His gospel.

Perseverance Under Pressure

The doctrine of Christ's return is also given to strengthen perseverance. Jesus warned His disciples about deception, hatred, betrayal, and tribulation before His coming, then said, "the one who has endured to the end, he will be saved" (Matt. 24:13). The apostles echo the same pattern. James says, "Be patient, brothers, until the presence of the Lord" and compares Christian endurance to the farmer waiting for precious fruit from the earth (Jas. 5:7–8). Paul tells the Thessalonians that their steadfastness under persecution is evidence of God's righteous judgment and that relief will come "at the revelation of the Lord Jesus from heaven" (2 Thess. 1:4–7). Revelation calls for "the endurance and the faith of the holy ones" in the face of beastly pressure (Rev. 13:10; 14:12).

This means the expectation of Christ's return is not an escape from suffering. It is the strength to endure suffering without surrender. The church does not wait for Christ by pretending difficulties do not exist. It waits by remaining faithful within them. The coming of Christ assures believers that evil is temporary, suffering is not ultimate, and the world's verdict is not final. The holy ones can therefore endure because they know the King will come.

Perseverance includes doctrinal steadfastness. In the last days many will be deceived. False teachers will arise. Lawlessness will increase. The love of many will grow cold (Matt. 24:11–12; 1 Tim. 4:1; 2 Tim. 3:1–5; 2 Pet. 2:1–3). Therefore readiness requires clinging to the truth. It is not enough to feel religious urgency. One must hold fast to the apostolic gospel, resist corruption, and refuse the spirit of antichrist. The one who watches is the one who remains loyal to truth and holiness until the appearing of the Lord.

Perseverance also includes courage. The world may mock the promise of Christ's return. Scoffers may say, "Where is the promise of His coming?" (2 Pet. 3:4). The faithful must not surrender to that mockery. The apparent stability of the present age is deceptive. The day of the Lord will come. The church must therefore continue in faith even when the world treats its hope as foolishness.

Edward D. Andrews

Living as Though He Returns Tomorrow

A faithful doctrine of readiness leads to a simple and powerful principle: live as though Jesus is returning tomorrow. This does not mean indulging in panic, abandoning responsibility, or pretending to know what Scripture has not revealed. It means maintaining righteous standing with God now. It means refusing to postpone repentance. It means doing the will of the Father today instead of assuming there will always be more time.

Jesus taught this spirit of readiness repeatedly. "You also prove yourselves ready, because at an hour that you do not think likely, the Son of Man is coming" (Matt. 24:44). The wise servant is ready because he is faithful when the master comes. The wise virgins are ready because they are prepared when the cry goes out. The ready disciple is not the one who has mastered a chart, but the one whose life is in order before God.

To live as though Christ may return tomorrow means maintaining a clean conscience through repentance and obedience. It means not carrying secret rebellion into another day. It means not excusing spiritual laziness. It means remaining in prayer, in truth, in worship, and in loyalty to God's Word. It means loving one's neighbor, forgiving others, speaking truthfully, honoring marriage, resisting impurity, and walking in the fear of God.

This kind of readiness does not shrink life into anxious minimalism. It gives life clarity. Because the return of Christ is certain and the day is unknown, each day matters. The believer does not postpone holiness to a later season. He seeks to be found faithful now.

Planning as Though It Is Fifty Years Away

At the same time, biblical readiness does not mean abandoning long-term responsibility. The same Scriptures that call for watchfulness also commend diligence, stewardship, provision, and wise planning. Proverbs says, "The plans of the diligent surely lead to advantage" (Prov. 21:5). Jesus told His hearers to count the cost before building a tower (Luke 14:28–30). Paul says that if anyone does not provide for his own household, he has denied the faith and is worse than an unbeliever (1 Tim. 5:8). He also rebukes those who had become disorderly, refusing to work, and commands quiet labor and responsible conduct (2 Thess. 3:6–12).

Readiness for Christ's return therefore does not forbid ordinary human planning. A Christian may pursue education, build a career, marry, raise children, buy a home, and make provision for the future. There is nothing unspiritual about faithful work, family life, or long-term responsibility. Indeed, these may be part of the very obedience Christ requires. A thirty-year mortgage is not a denial of the Second Coming. Raising children is not a compromise with watchfulness. Learning a trade, developing skill, or planning wisely for future responsibilities is not worldliness in itself.

The issue is not whether one plans. The issue is what governs the planning. Jesus condemned anxious and idolatrous living that seeks first material security while neglecting the kingdom of God (Matt. 6:25–34). James rebuked arrogant planners who spoke as though the future were theirs to control, forgetting that their life is a vapor and that they ought to say, "If Jehovah wills, we will live and also do this or that" (Jas. 4:13–15). Scripture therefore does not forbid planning. It forbids planning that becomes proud, self-sufficient, or detached from the will of God.

The balanced Christian life may therefore be described this way: live as though Jesus is returning tomorrow, and plan as though ordinary responsibilities may continue for many years. The first guards holiness. The second guards stability. The first prevents procrastinated obedience. The second prevents irresponsible fanaticism. Together they reflect the wisdom of Scripture.

Family, Work, and Education Under the Kingdom

This balance becomes especially important in everyday life. Marriage is honorable and belongs to God's good order (Gen. 2:18–24; Heb. 13:4). Children are a gift from Jehovah (Ps. 127:3–5). Honest labor is honorable and necessary (Eph. 4:28; 1 Thess. 4:11–12). Growth in skill, wisdom, and understanding is valuable when pursued in the fear of God (Prov. 1:7; 4:5–9). None of these things stands opposed to readiness for Christ's return when kept in proper place.

The danger lies in disordered priorities. Jesus warned that the worries of this age, the deceitfulness of riches, and the desires for other things can choke the Word and make it unfruitful (Mark 4:19). He warned against laying up treasure on earth as though permanence could be found there (Matt. 6:19–21). He said plainly, "keep on seeking first the kingdom and His righteousness" (Matt. 6:33). The believer may therefore build a household, pursue useful work, and make wise plans, but none of these may become the center of life. They must remain subordinate to the will of the Father.

This is what it means to live responsibly without becoming earthbound in the wrong sense. The Christian is not called to despise ordinary responsibilities. He is called to hold them in their proper place. Family is a stewardship, not an idol. Work is a duty, not a master. Education is a tool, not an ultimate goal. Property is a trust, not a kingdom. The coming of Christ relativizes all these things without abolishing them.

The believer who understands this will neither neglect his responsibilities nor worship them. He will marry in the Lord, raise children in the discipline of the Lord, work honestly before the Lord, and make plans under the lordship of Christ. In doing so he lives as one who knows the world is passing away, yet who also knows that present obedience includes faithful stewardship of present callings.

Readiness in Prayer, Worship, and Fellowship

Living in readiness also requires a life shaped by prayer, worship, and fellowship with God's people. Jesus told His disciples to keep on the watch and pray (Luke 21:36). Peter says that because the end of all things has drawn close, believers must be "sound in mind and self-controlled with a view to prayers" (1 Pet. 4:7). Prayer keeps the heart awake. It reminds the believer that life is lived before God and not merely before men. It resists the self-sufficiency that grows out of worldly planning detached from dependence upon Jehovah.

Worship also belongs at the center of readiness. The church proclaims the Lord's death "until He comes" (1 Cor. 11:26). The gathered life of believers is therefore future-oriented. The congregation remembers what Christ accomplished and looks forward to what He will complete.

In worship, the church learns again who God is, who Christ is, what truth is, and where history is going. This steadies the mind against deception and the heart against compromise.

Fellowship with the holy ones is equally necessary. Hebrews urges believers not to forsake their own gathering together, "and all the more so as you see the day drawing near" (Heb. 10:25). The nearer the day, the more necessary mutual exhortation becomes. The Christian who tries to await Christ in isolation places himself in danger. Readiness is strengthened in the fellowship of truth, prayer, worship, correction, and encouragement.

The Steady Life of the Awaiting Church

The church that truly lives in expectation of Christ's return will be marked by a particular kind of steadiness. It will not be swept away by every rumor, nor will it be lulled to sleep by the apparent permanence of the world. It will not become lazy because the Lord has not yet appeared, nor will it become reckless because He may appear soon. It will be sober, obedient, diligent, hopeful, and watchful.

Such a church will love holiness because the King is holy. It will labor faithfully because the Master will return. It will preach the gospel because Judgment Day is fixed. It will endure because suffering is temporary. It will make wise plans because present obedience requires stewardship. It will hold those plans loosely because the kingdom of God is its true future. It will remain in prayer because the Lord may come at any hour. It will remain in truth because deception increases as the end draws near.

This is the life of readiness Scripture commands. It is not sensational. It is not careless. It is not suspended between fear and excitement. It is settled under the Word of God. It lives each day under the lordship of Christ and each year under the providential permission of God, without allowing long-term responsibilities to crowd out eternal priorities.

The final prayer of Scripture remains the church's own: "Amen. Come, Lord Jesus" (Rev. 22:20). But that prayer is not an excuse to abandon the duties of today. It is the cry of a people who watch, work, worship, endure, and obey until He comes. The certainty of Christ's return therefore does not pull the faithful out of life. It teaches them how to live it rightly—awake, clean, useful, steadfast, and always ready for the appearing of the King.

Edward D. Andrews

Glossary of Terms

Antichrist

A doctrinal and spiritual opponent of Christ, especially one who denies the truth about Jesus Christ. In Scripture, antichrist is not limited to one simplified figure, but includes many present deceivers while also pointing toward the final concentration of anti-Christ rebellion.

Apostasy

A deliberate falling away from revealed truth within the professing sphere of faith. In the context of the Second Coming, apostasy precedes the full unveiling of lawlessness and marks the maturing rebellion of the last days.

Appearance of His Coming

Paul's expression for the public manifestation of Christ in glory by which He destroys the lawless one. It emphasizes that Christ's return is visible, historical, and decisive.

Beast

The anti-God imperial power portrayed especially in Revelation as the concentrated political-religious order energized by Satan. It opposes God, persecutes the holy ones, demands allegiance, and is destroyed at Christ's coming.

Blessed Hope

The sure expectation of the appearing of Jesus Christ in glory. It is not speculative curiosity about the future, but the church's confident expectation of resurrection, judgment, kingdom, and restoration.

Day of the Lord

The climactic day of divine intervention in judgment and salvation. In New Testament teaching, it is bound up with the return of Christ, the overthrow of evil, and the transition into the next stage of God's kingdom purpose.

Everlasting Life

The enduring life granted by God to the righteous through Christ. In this book's framework, everlasting life is the gift given to the broader righteous under God's kingdom, distinguished from the immortality granted to the first-resurrection reigning company.

Final Judgment

God's righteous and public judgment of all mankind through Jesus Christ. It brings final exposure of rebellion, vindication of the righteous, and the appointed end of the wicked.

First Resurrection

The resurrection identified in Revelation 20 as belonging to the blessed and holy company who reign with Christ for a thousand years. Those who share in it are priests of God and of Christ, and over them the second death has no authority.

Glorified Christ

Jesus Christ after His resurrection, ascension, and exaltation, now reigning in heavenly glory and destined to return openly in power and judgment.

Great Apostasy

The broad defection from revealed truth that precedes the day of the Lord. It forms the spiritual setting in which the man of lawlessness is revealed.

Great White Throne

The final judgment scene of Revelation 20 in which the dead are judged before God after the thousand years and the final rebellion.

Heavenly Calling

The divine calling associated with the holy ones who share in the first resurrection and reign with Christ. In this framework, it is connected with priestly and royal service in the millennial administration.

Holy Ones

God's people set apart to Him through Christ. In prophetic context, the holy ones are persecuted by beastly power, vindicated by resurrection, and ultimately inherit the kingdom under the reign of Christ.

Immortality

Deathless life in the fullest Pauline sense. In this book's framework, immortality is especially associated with the first-resurrection company who reign with Christ, rather than being applied indiscriminately to all the saved.

Judgment Day

The appointed day on which God judges the inhabited earth in righteousness through His Son. It is fixed, certain, and inseparable from the return of Christ.

Kingdom of God

God's righteous rule manifested through His Messiah. In relation to the Second Coming, the kingdom is openly advanced through Christ's return, the destruction of anti-God power, the millennial reign, and the final renewal.

Lawless One / Man of Lawlessness

The concentrated expression of apostate rebellion described in 2 Thessalonians 2. He exalts himself in the sphere of worship, is associated with deception and false signs, and is destroyed by Christ's appearing.

Mark of the Beast

The sign of allegiance to the beastly order, associated with loyalty in thought and action. It marks participation in the anti-God system and stands over against belonging to God.

Millennial Reign

The thousand-year reign of Christ described in Revelation 20. It begins after Christ's visible return, after the destruction of the beast and false prophet, and before the final release of Satan, the last rebellion, and the great white throne judgment.

New Heaven and New Earth

The fully renewed order that follows final judgment. It is the sphere of everlasting righteousness, divine presence, and the removal of death, sorrow, and curse.

Parousia

A New Testament term for the coming or presence of Christ. In this book, it refers to His one visible, public, and glorious return rather than a secret or divided coming.

Premillennialism

The biblical understanding that Christ returns before the thousand-year reign. According to this view, Christ appears, the anti-God order is judged, Satan is bound, the holy ones reign with Christ, and only afterward come the final rebellion and final judgment.

Resurrection

God's raising of the dead through the power of Christ. Scripture presents resurrection, not the survival of an immortal soul, as the believer's great hope and the divine answer to death.

Second Coming

The literal, visible, historical return of Jesus Christ in glory. It is not a secret rapture, an inward spiritual experience, or merely a symbol of religious triumph, but the real return of the risen Lord.

Second Death

The final and irreversible judgment described in Revelation. It has no authority over those who share in the first resurrection.

Satan

The adversary, deceiver, and accuser who stands behind the anti-God order. He empowers rebellion in the present age, is bound during the millennium, released briefly after the thousand years, and finally destroyed under God's judgment.

Thousand Years

The defined kingdom period of Revelation 20 during which Christ reigns, the first-resurrection company reigns with Him, and Satan is bound from deceiving the nations in the former sense.

Tribulation

A time of distress, pressure, and persecution associated with the conflict between the kingdom of God and the anti-God order. In this book's setting, tribulation is connected with endurance, faithfulness, and final vindication at Christ's return.

Visible Return

The public and unmistakable appearing of Christ. This term emphasizes that His coming is seen, manifested, and historically real, not hidden or symbolic.

Watchfulness

The believer's posture of readiness, faithfulness, and holiness in light of the certainty of Christ's return. Watchfulness rejects both date-setting sensationalism and careless indifference.

Wrath to Come

The coming divine judgment from which believers are delivered through Christ. It includes the outpouring of judgment upon the wicked and the overthrow of the present evil order.

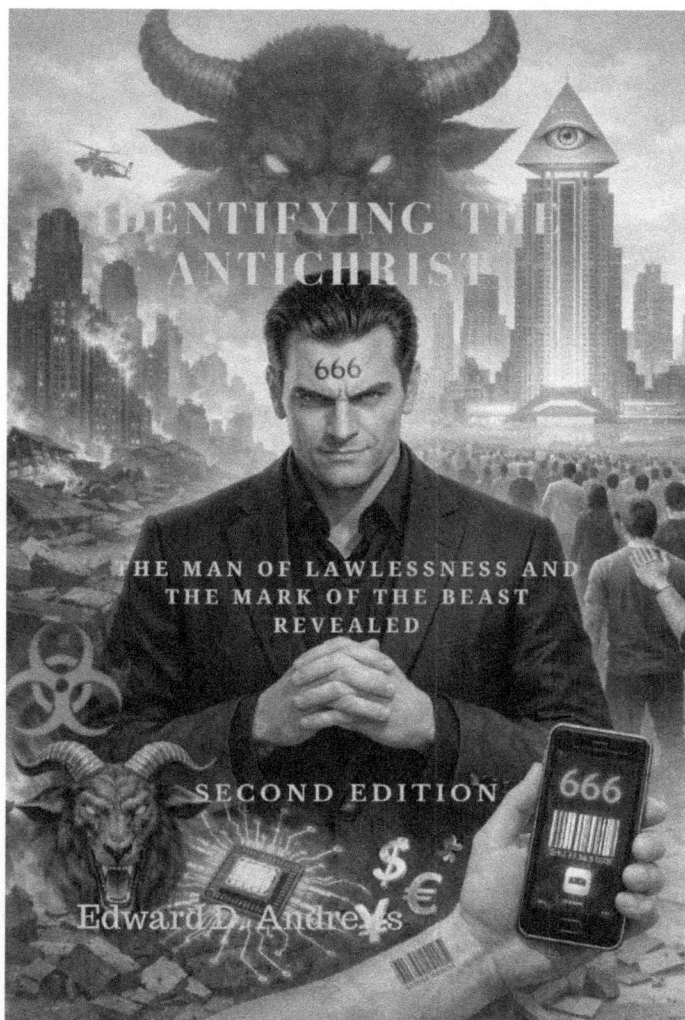

Edward D. Andrews

Edward D. Andrews

REVELATION

A Historical-Grammatical Exegetical
Commentary on the Apocalypse, the Kingdom
of God, and the Final Triumph of God

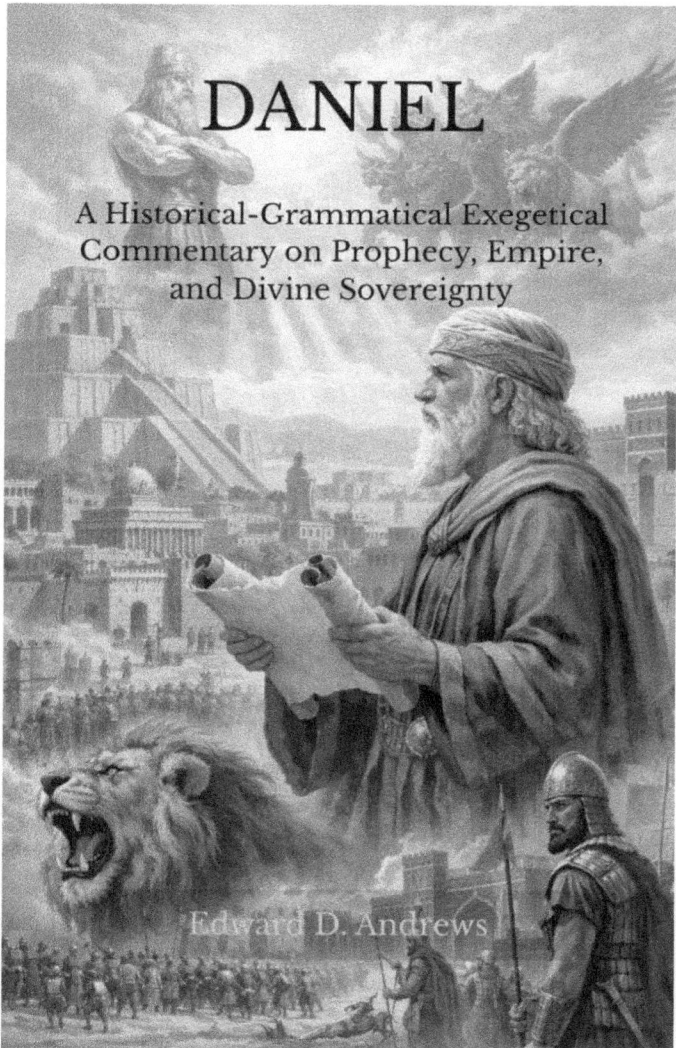

DANIEL

A Historical-Grammatical Exegetical
Commentary on Prophecy, Empire,
and Divine Sovereignty

Edward D. Andrews

Bibliography

Akin, D. L. (2001). *The New American Commentary: 1, 2, 3 John*. Nashville, TN: Broadman & Holman .

Aland, K., Black, M., & Martini, C. M. (1993; 2006). *The Greek New Testament, Fourth Revised Edition (Interlinear With Morphology)*. Deutsche Bibelgesellschaft: United Bible Society.

Andrews, E. D. (2016). *INTERPRETING THE BIBLE: Introduction to Biblical Hermeneutics*. Cambridge, OH: Christian Publishing House.

Andrews, E. D. (2017). *FEARLESS: Be Courageous and Strong Through Your Faith In These Last Days*. Cambridge, OH: Christian Publishing House.

Andrews, E. D. (2017). *GOD WILL GET YOU THROUGH THIS: Hope and Help for Your Difficult Times*. Cambridge, OH: Christian Publishing House.

Andrews, E. D. (2017). *HOW TO STUDY YOUR BIBLE: Rightly Handling the Word of God*. Cambridge, OH: Christian Publishing House.

Andrews, E. D. (2017). *HUMAN IMPERFECTION: While We Were Sinners Christ Died For Us*. Cambridge, OH: Christian Ppublishing House.

Andrews, E. D. (2017). *IDENTIFYING THE ANTICHRIST: The Man of Lawlessness and the Mark of the Beast Revealed*. Cambridge, OH: Christian Publishing House.

Andrews, E. D. (2018). *BLESSED BY GOD IN SATAN'S WORLD: How All Things Are Working for Your Good.* Cambridge, OH: Christian Publishing House.

Andrews, E. D. (2018). *REASONABLE FAITH: Saving Those Who Doubt.* Cambridge, OH: Christian Publishing House.

Andrews, E. D. (2018). *REASONING FROM THE SCRIPTURES: Sharing CHRIST as You Help Others to Learn about the Mighty works of God.* Cambridge, Ohio: Christian Publishing House.

Andrews, E. D. (2019). *SATAN: Know Your Enemy.* Cambridge, OH: Christian Publishing House.

Andrews, E. D. (2023). *BIBLICAL APOCALYPTICS HANDBOOK: A Study of the Most Important Revelations that God and Christ Disclosed in the Bible.* Cambridge, OH: Christian Publishing House.

Andrews, E. D. (2023). *BIBLICAL EXEGESIS: Biblical Criticism on Trial.* Cambridge, OH: Christian Publishing House.

Andrews, E. D. (2023). *CHRISTIAN APOLOGETICS: Answering the Tough Questions: Evidence and Reason in Defense of the Faith.* Cambridge, Ohio: Christian Publishing House.

Andrews, E. D. (2023). *HOW WE GOT THE BIBLE.* Cambridge, OH: Christian Publishing House.

Andrews, E. D. (2024). *CHRISTIAN THEOLOGY: The Christian's Ultimate Guide to Learning from the Bible.* Cambridge, OH: Christian Publishing House.

Andrews, E. D. (2024). *REASON MEETS FAITH: Addressing and Refuting Atheism's Challenges to*

Christianity. Cambridge, OH: Christian Publishing House.

Andrews, E. D. (2025). *A FRESH LOOK AT PAUL'S THEOLOGY: Biblical Theology as Revealed through Paul.* Cambridge, OH: Christian Publishing House.

Andrews, E. D. (2025). *BIBLICAL WORDS AND THEIR MEANING: An Introduction to Lexical Semantics.* Cambridge, OH: Christian Publishing House.

Andrews, E. D. (2025). *CAN WE TRUST THE BIBLE?* Cambridge, OH: Christian Publishing House.

Andrews, E. D. (2025). *THE ANDREWS BIBLE BLUEPRINT: Unlocking Scripture's Truth, History, and Wisdom.* Cambridge, OH: Christian Publishing House.

Andrews, E. D. (2025). *THE APOSTLE PAUL: Teacher, Preacher, Apologist, and Evangelist.* Cambridge, OH: Christian Publishing House.

Andrews, E. D. (2025). *THE GUIDE TO SPIRITUAL WARFARE: Standing Firm in the Armor of God Against the Schemes of the Devil.* Cambridge, OH: Christian Publishing House.

Andrews, E. D. (2025). *THE LAST WATCHMAN: Standing for Truth in a Fallen World.* Cambridge, OH: Christian Publishing House.

Andrews, E. D. (2025). *THE WAR AGAINST THE TRUTH: Exposing the Lies That Allegedly Undermine the Christian Faith.* Cambridge, OH: Christian Publishing House.

Andrews, E. D. (2026). *DANIEL: A Historical-Grammatical Exegetical Commentary on Prophecy, Empire, and Divine*

Sovereignty. Cambridge, OH: Christian Publishing House.

Andrews, E. D. (2026). *REVELATION: A Historical-Grammatical Exegetical Commentary on the Apocalypse, the Kingdom of God, and the Final Triumph of God.* Cambridge, OH: Christian Publishing House.

Barnes, A. (1884-85). *Barnes On Revelation: Albert Barnes' Notes On The Whole Bible.* London: Blackie & Son.

Collins, ,. J. (1994). *Daniel: A Commentary on the Book of Daniel.* Minneapolis, MN: Fortress Press.

Easley, K. H. (1999). *Holman New Testament Commentary - Revelation (Volume 12).* Nashville, TN: Broadman & Holman.

Ian, P. (2018). *Revelation: An Introduction and Commentary (Volume 20).* Downers Grove, Il: InterVarsity Press.

Miller, S. (1994). *Daniel (New American Commentary, 18).* Nashville, TN: Broadman & Holman Reference.

Thomas, R. L. (1992). *Revelation 1-7: An Exegetical Commentary* . Chicago, IL: Moody Publishers.

Thomas, R. L. (1995). *Revelation 8-22: An Exegetical Commentary* . Chicago, IL: Moody Publishers.

Walvoord, J. F. (2012). *Daniel (The John Walvoord Prophecy Commentaries).* Chicago, IL: Moody Publishers.

www.ingramcontent.com/pod-product-compliance
Lightning Source LLC
LaVergne TN
LVHW011223080426
835509LV00005B/287